HOW TO DRAW BOOK FOR GIRLS

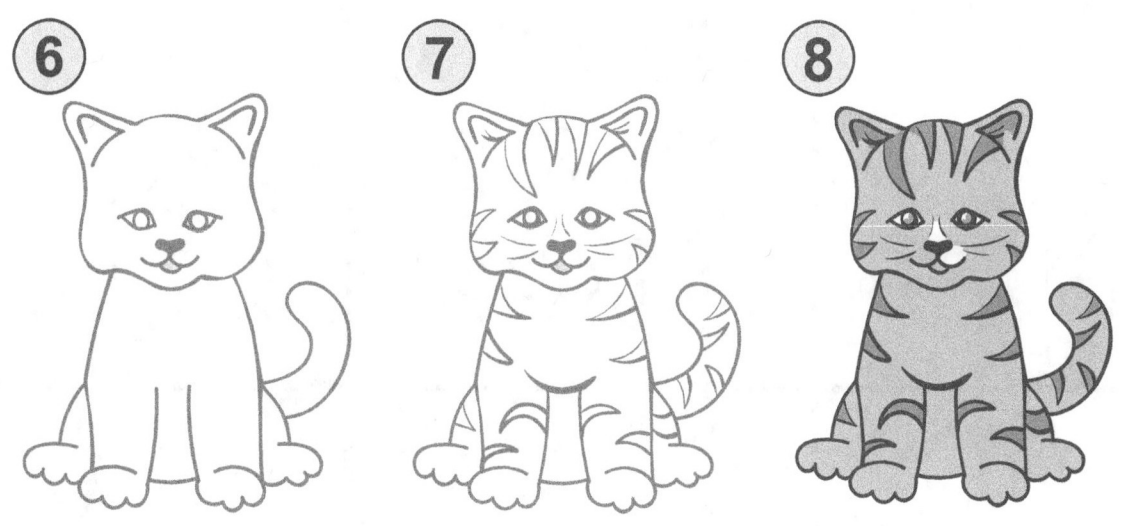

– RUSS FOCUS –

ISBN-13: 978-1725194335   ISBN-10: 1725194333

PUBLISHED BY RUSS FOCUS COPYRIGHT © 2018 ALL RIGHTS RESERVED
NO PART OF THIS PUBLICATION MAY BE REPRODUCED IN ANY
FORM OR BY ANY MEANS WITHOUT WRITTEN PERMISSION OF THE PUBLISHER.
WE ARE NOT RESPONSIBLE FOR UNSOLICITES MATERIAL PUBLISHED IN USA

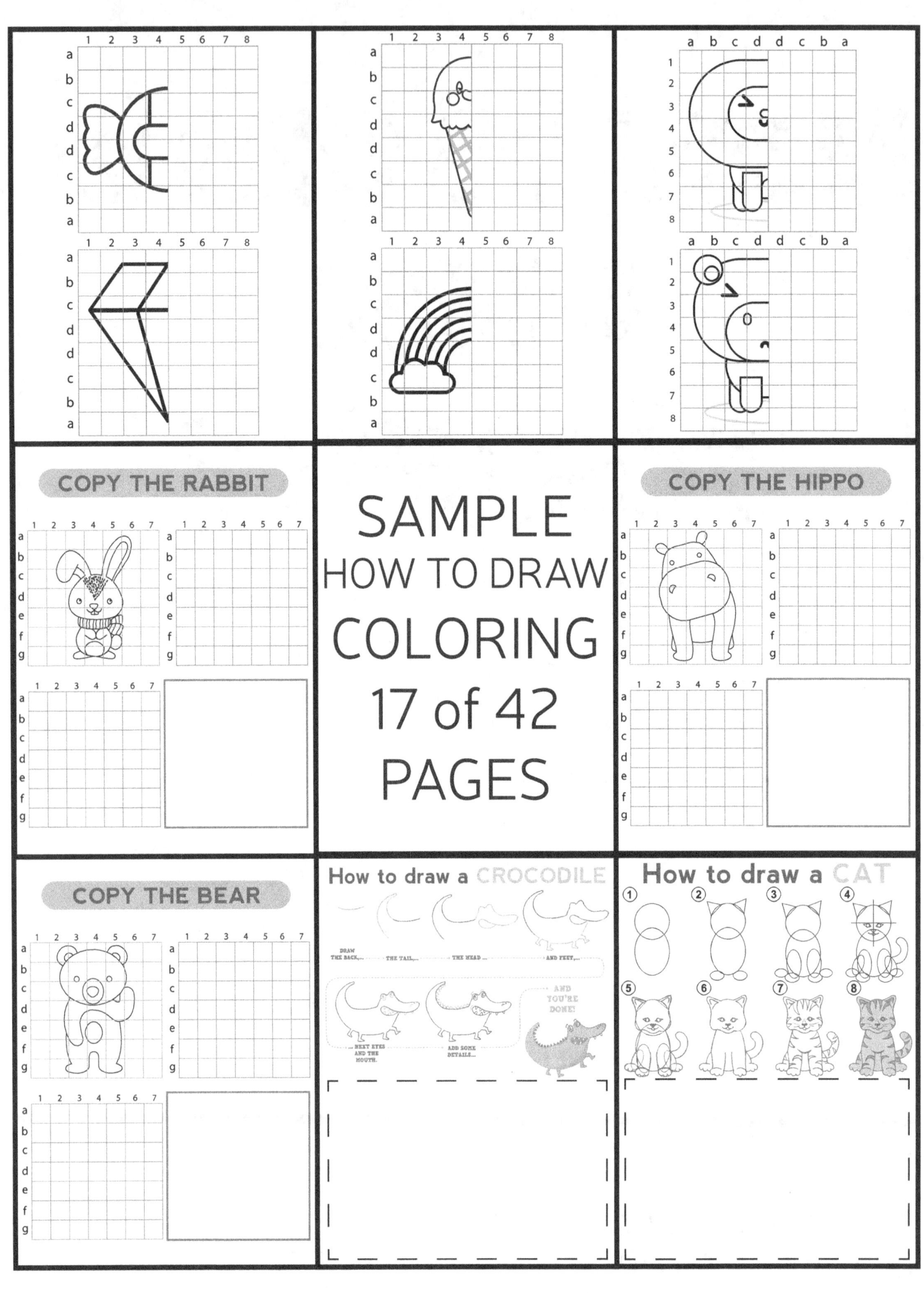

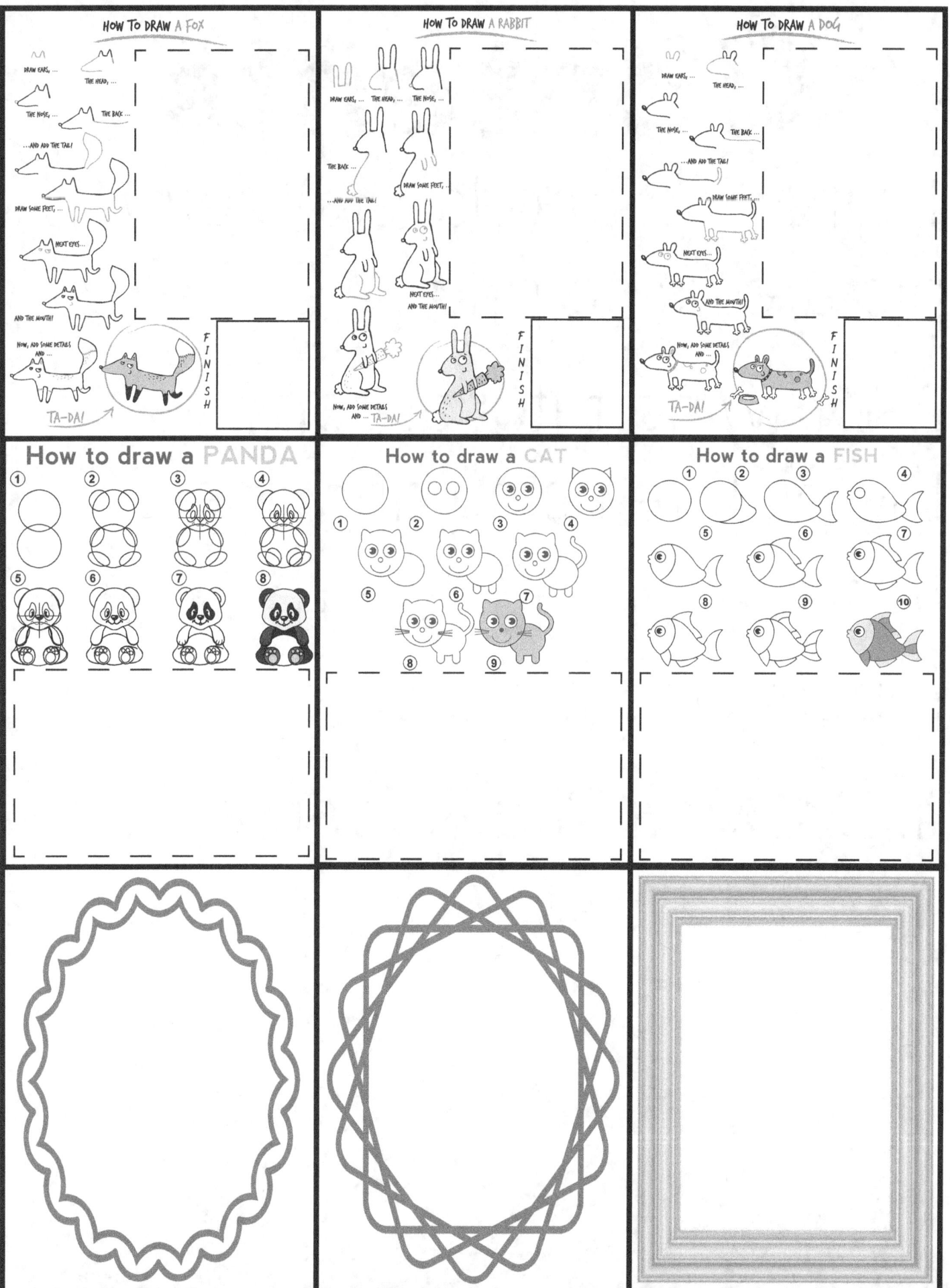

Contents

1. Drawing tutorial simmetry picture using grid.

2. Drawing tutorial copy the picture using grid lines.

3. Drawing tutorial step by step repeats the picture.

4. Drawing Pad & Frame.

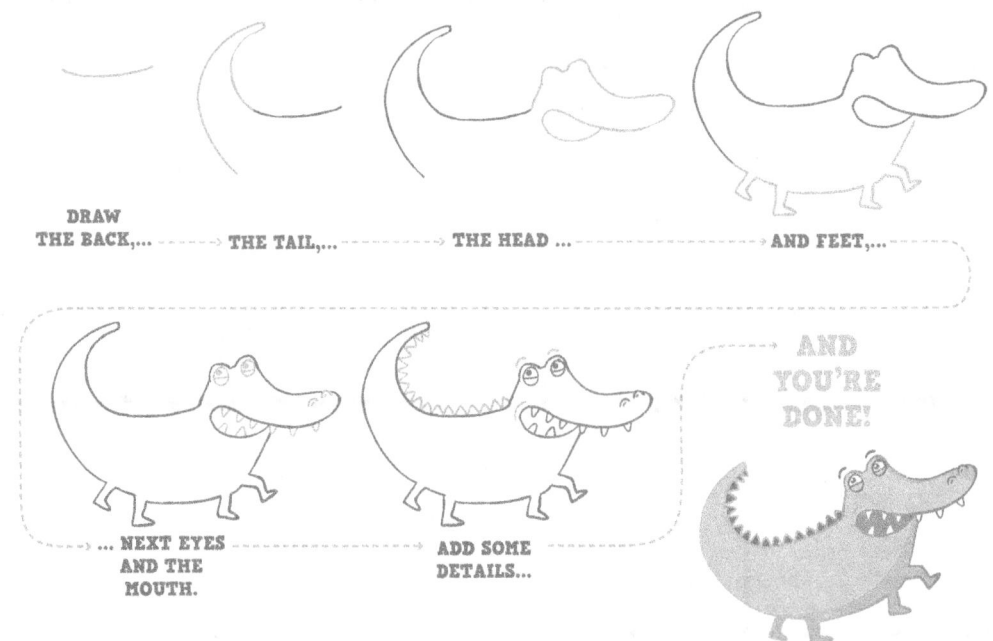

www.russfocus.com

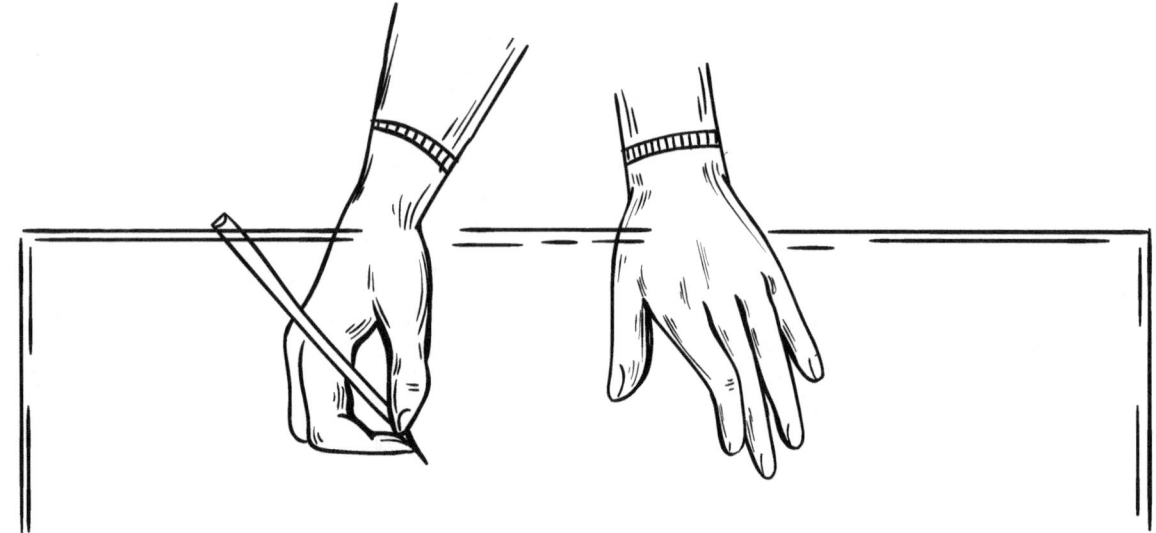

Drawing tutorial simmetry picture using grid.

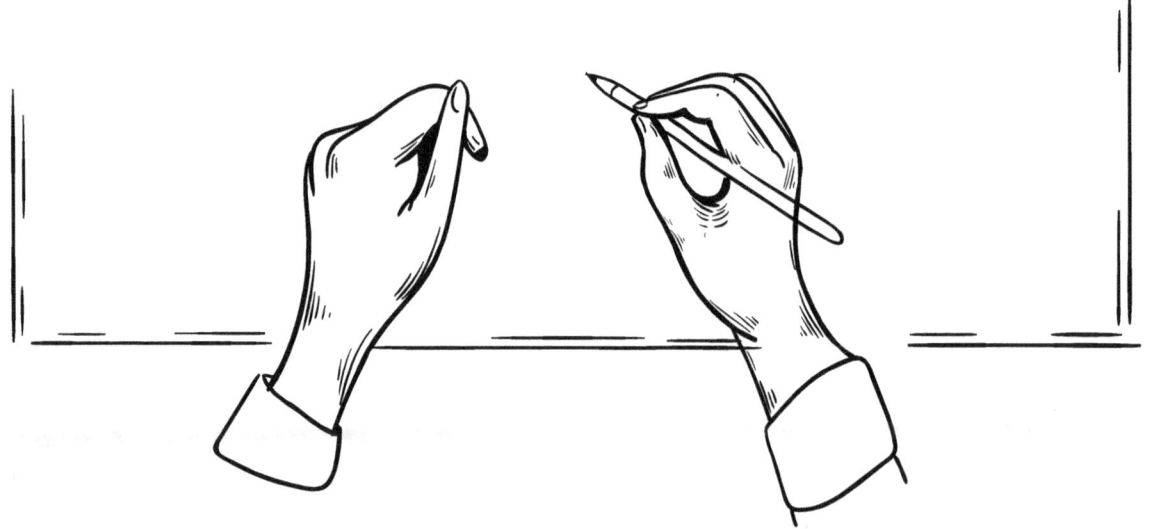

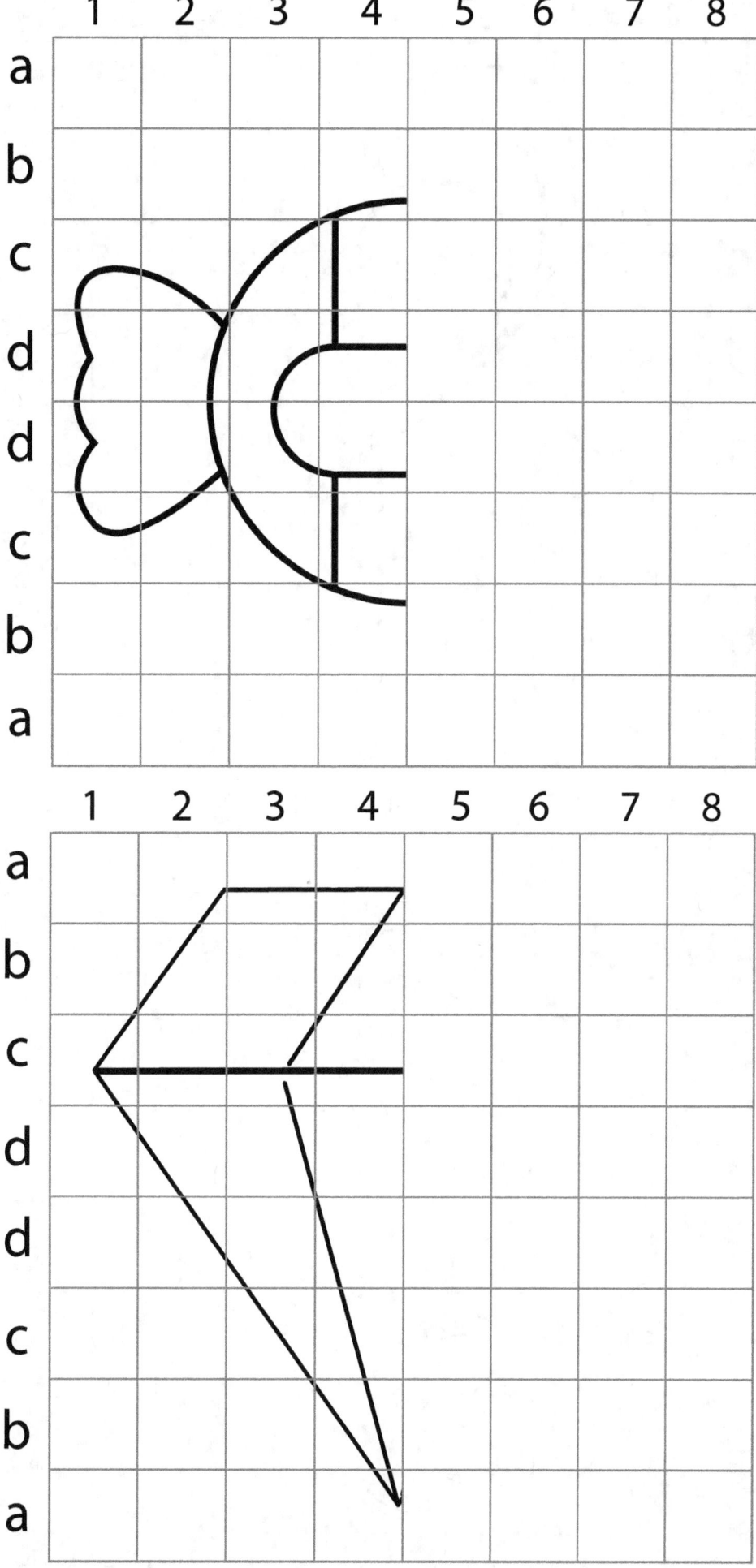

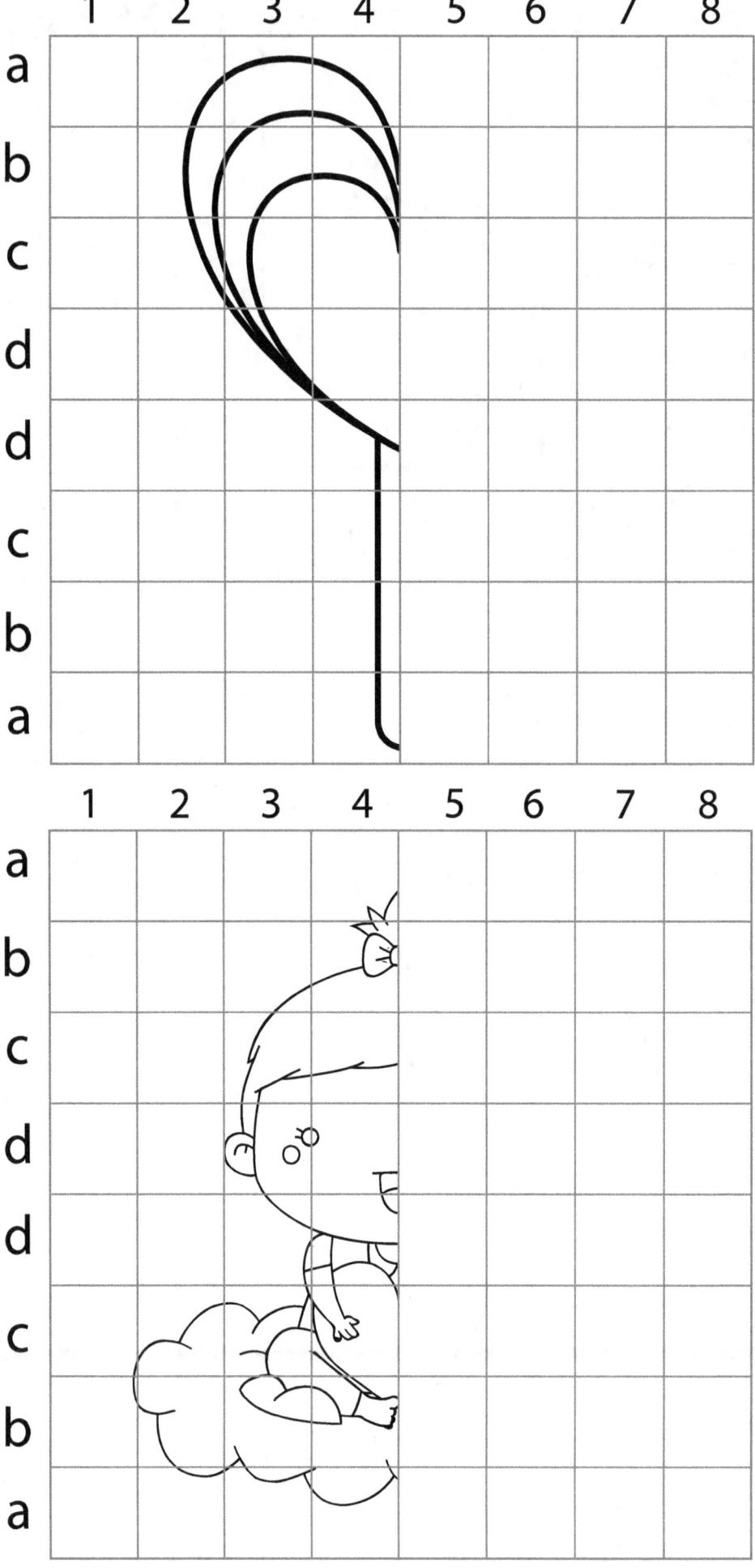

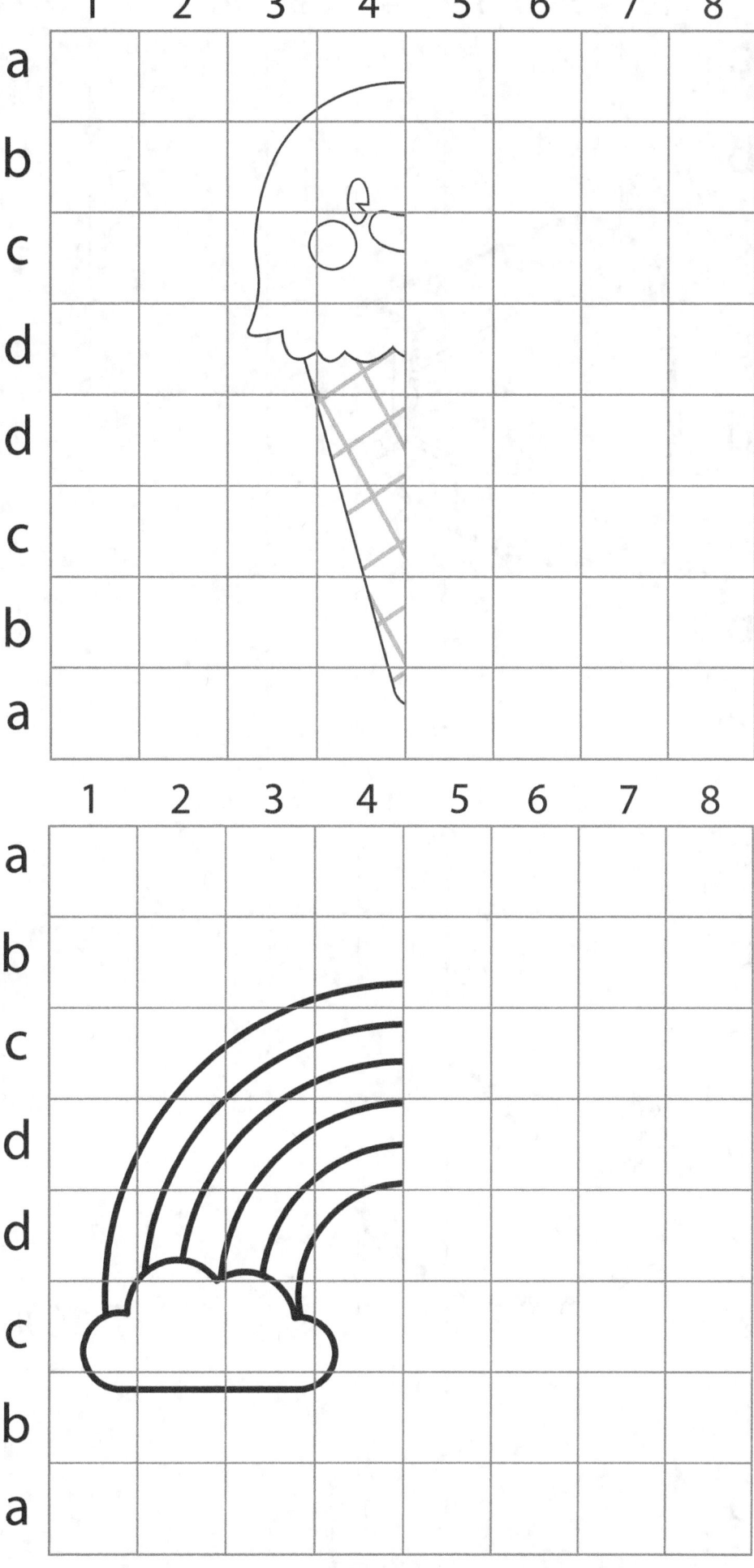

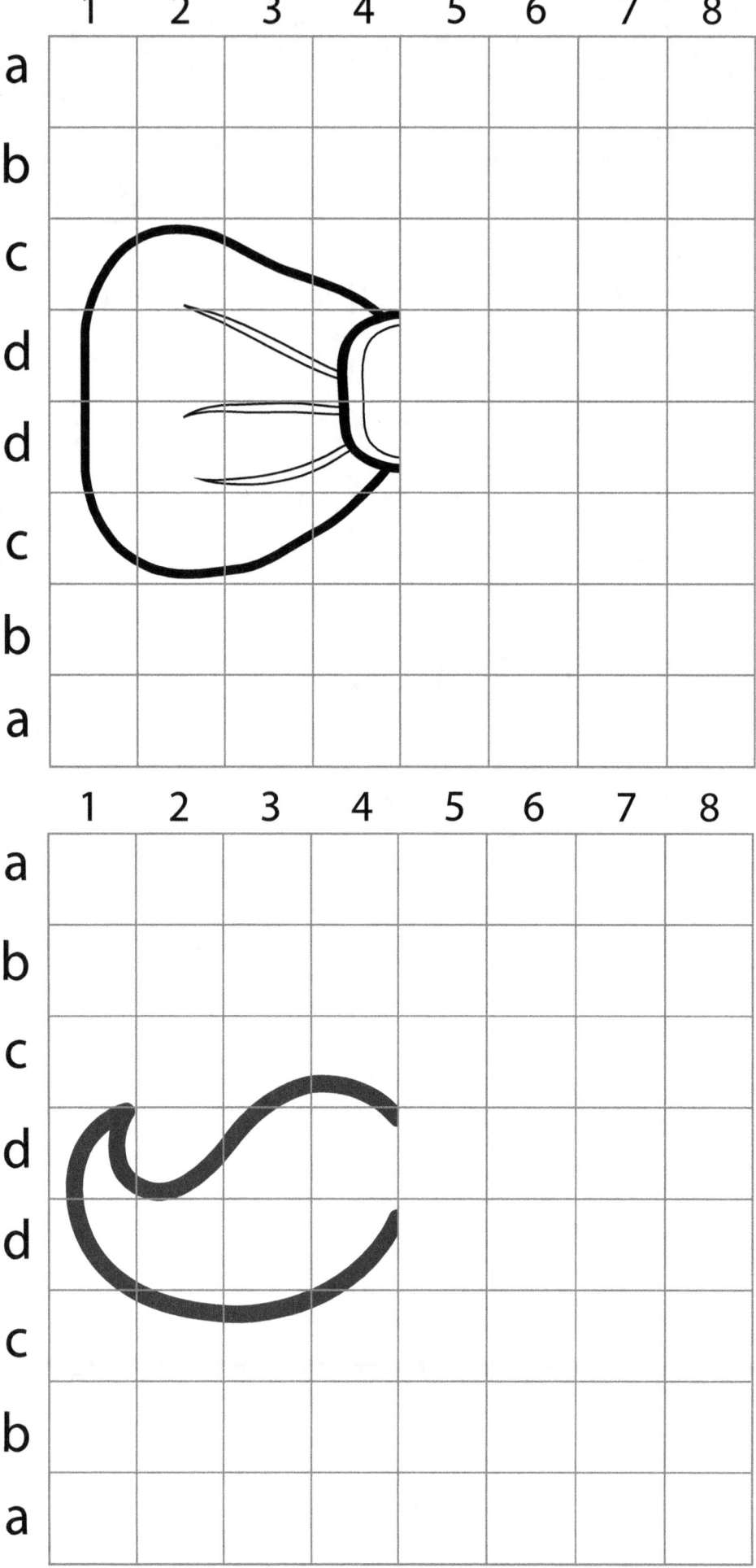

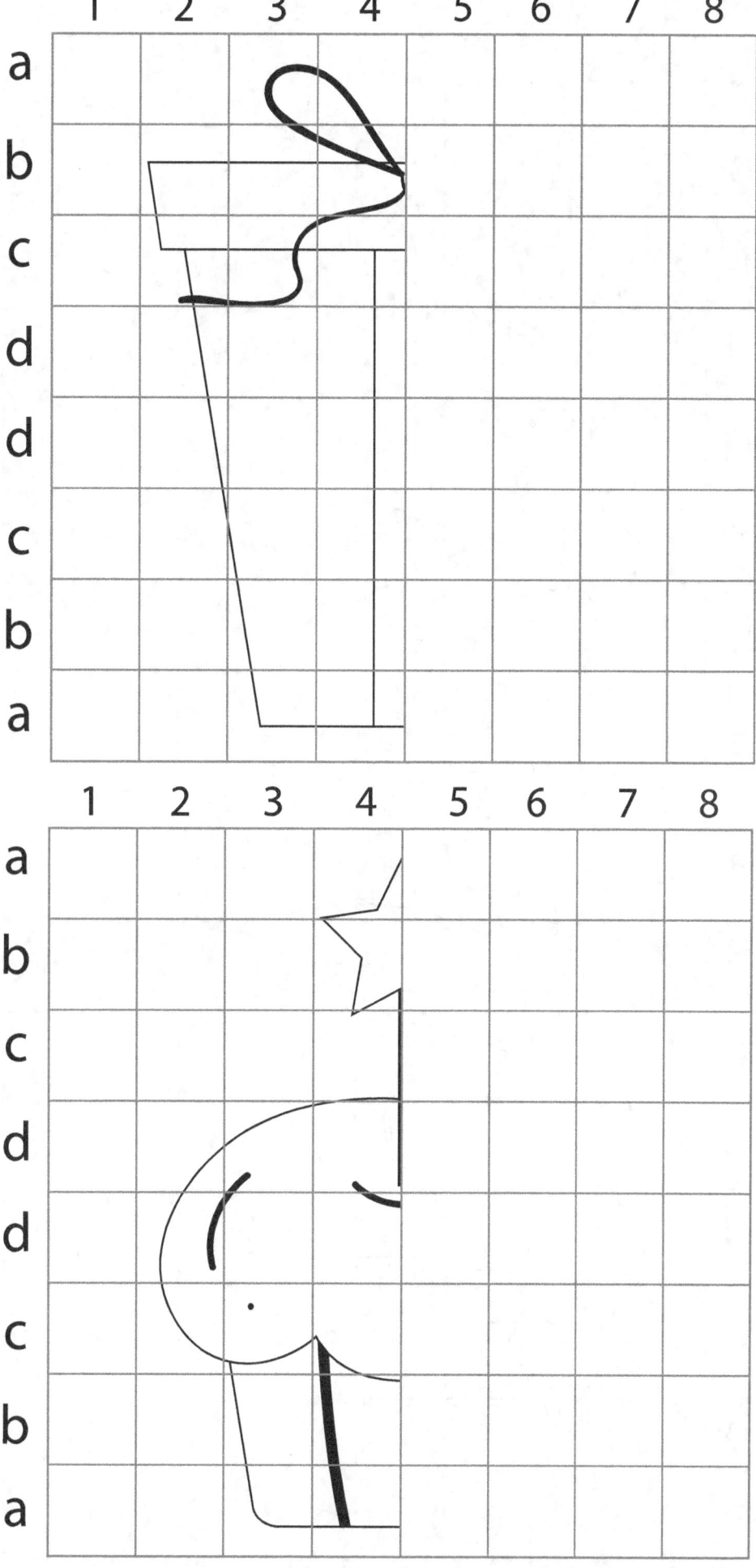

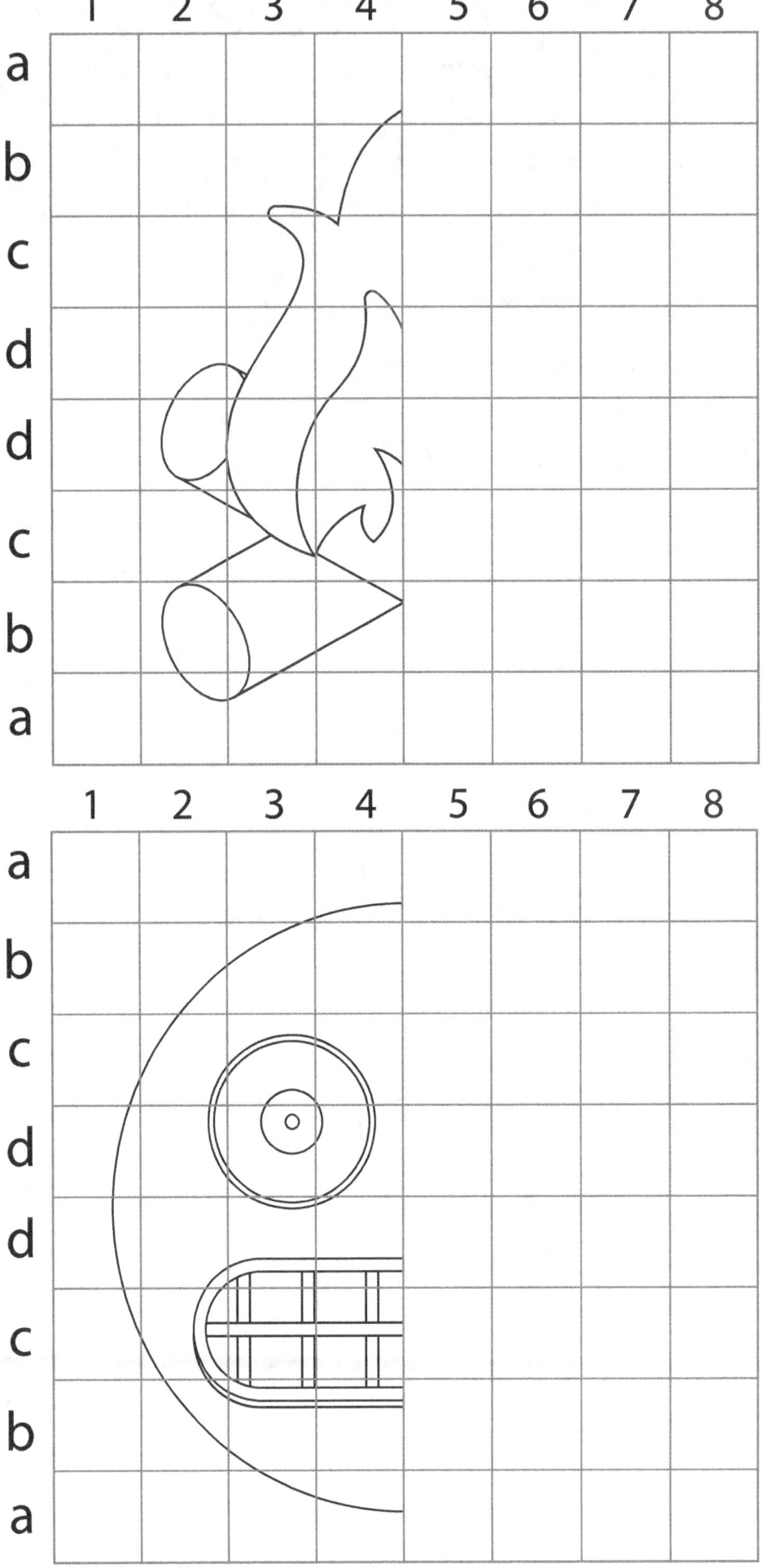

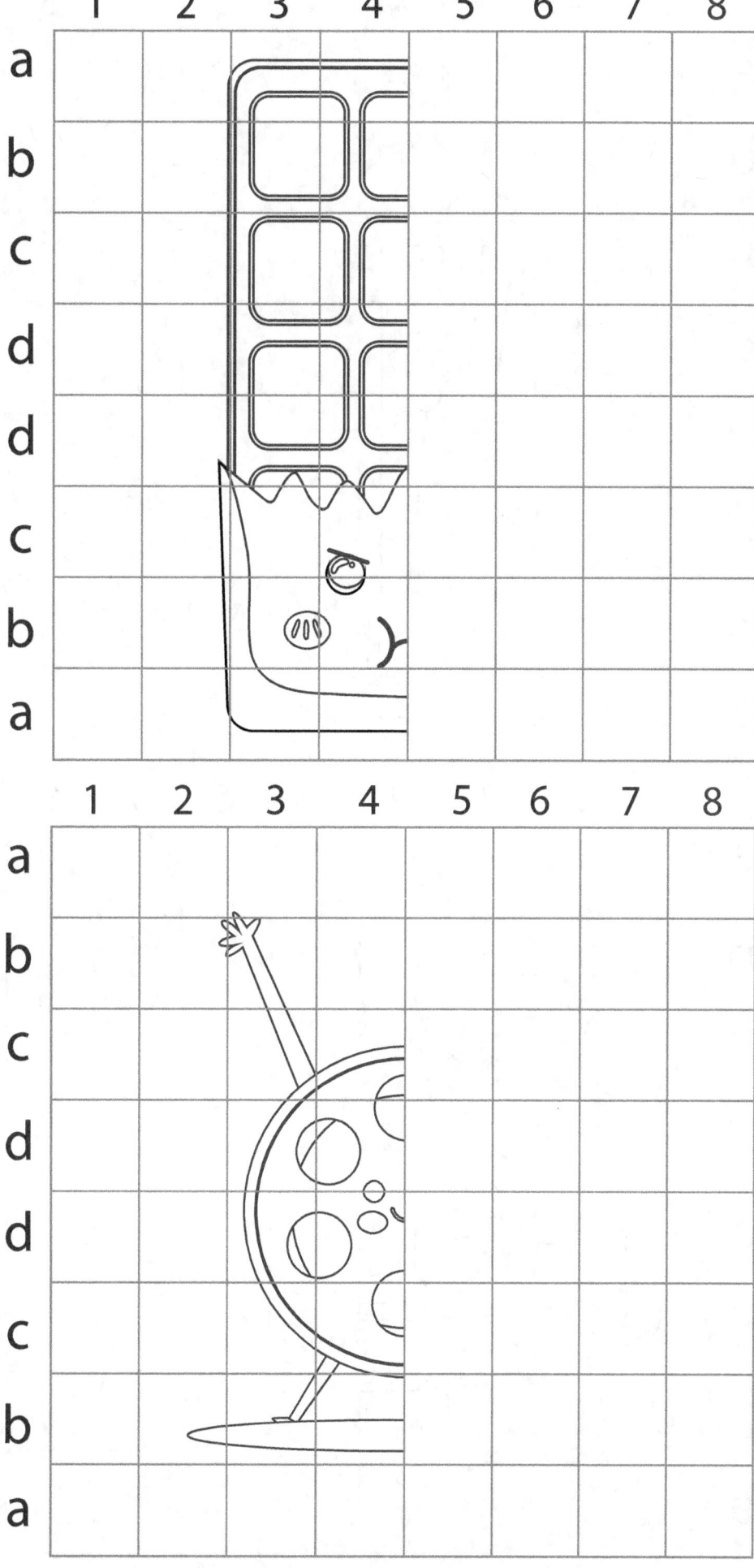

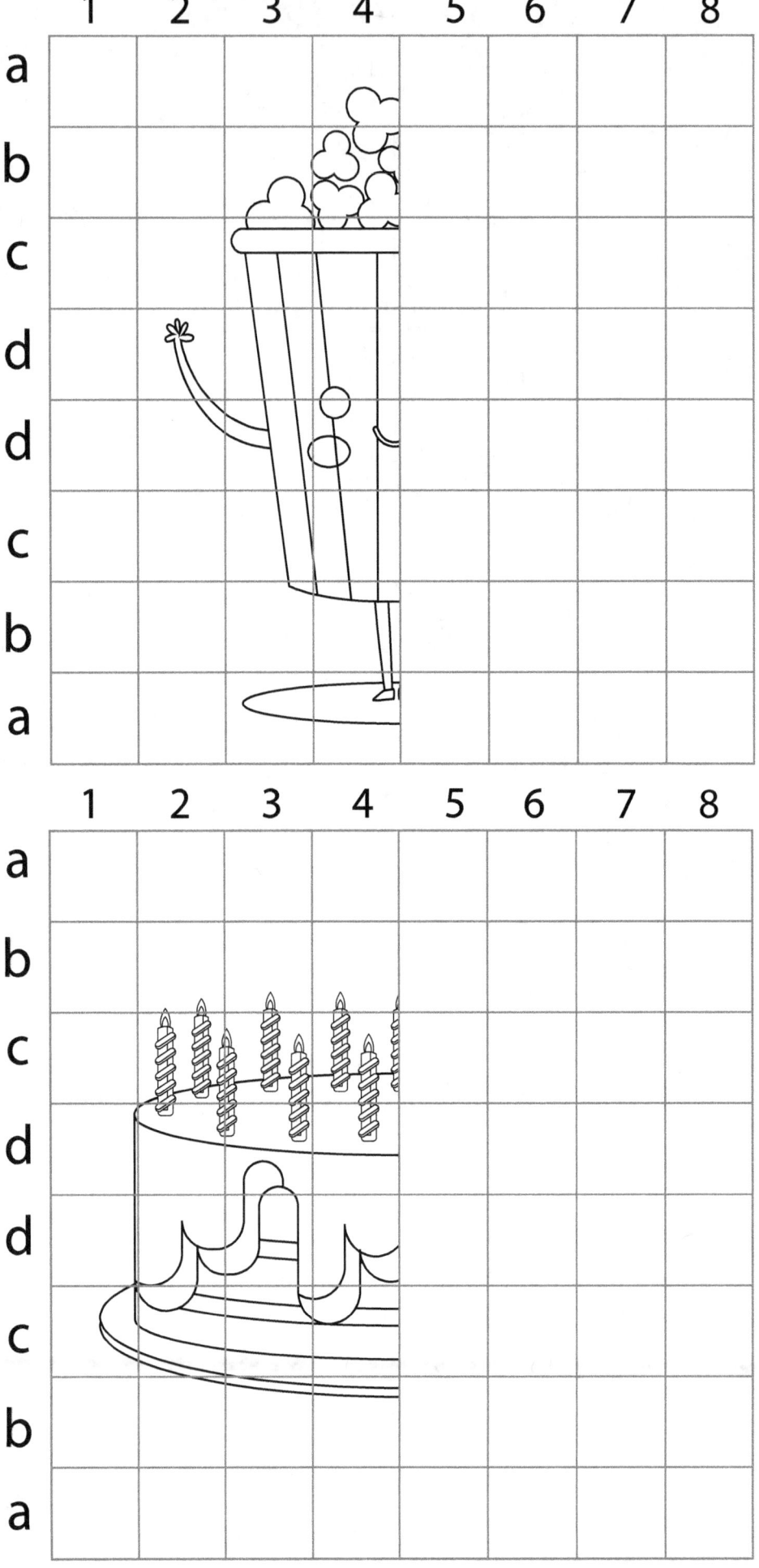

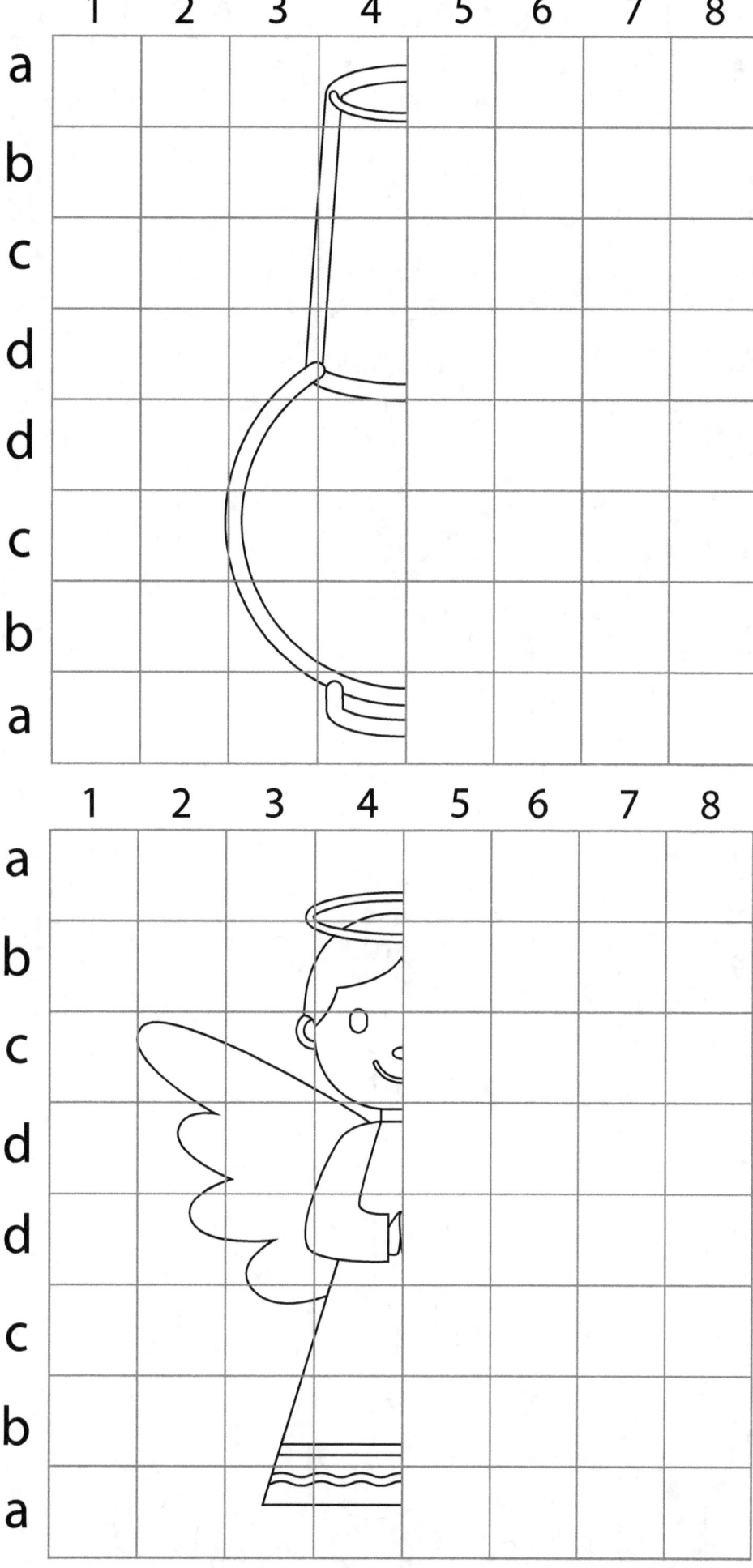

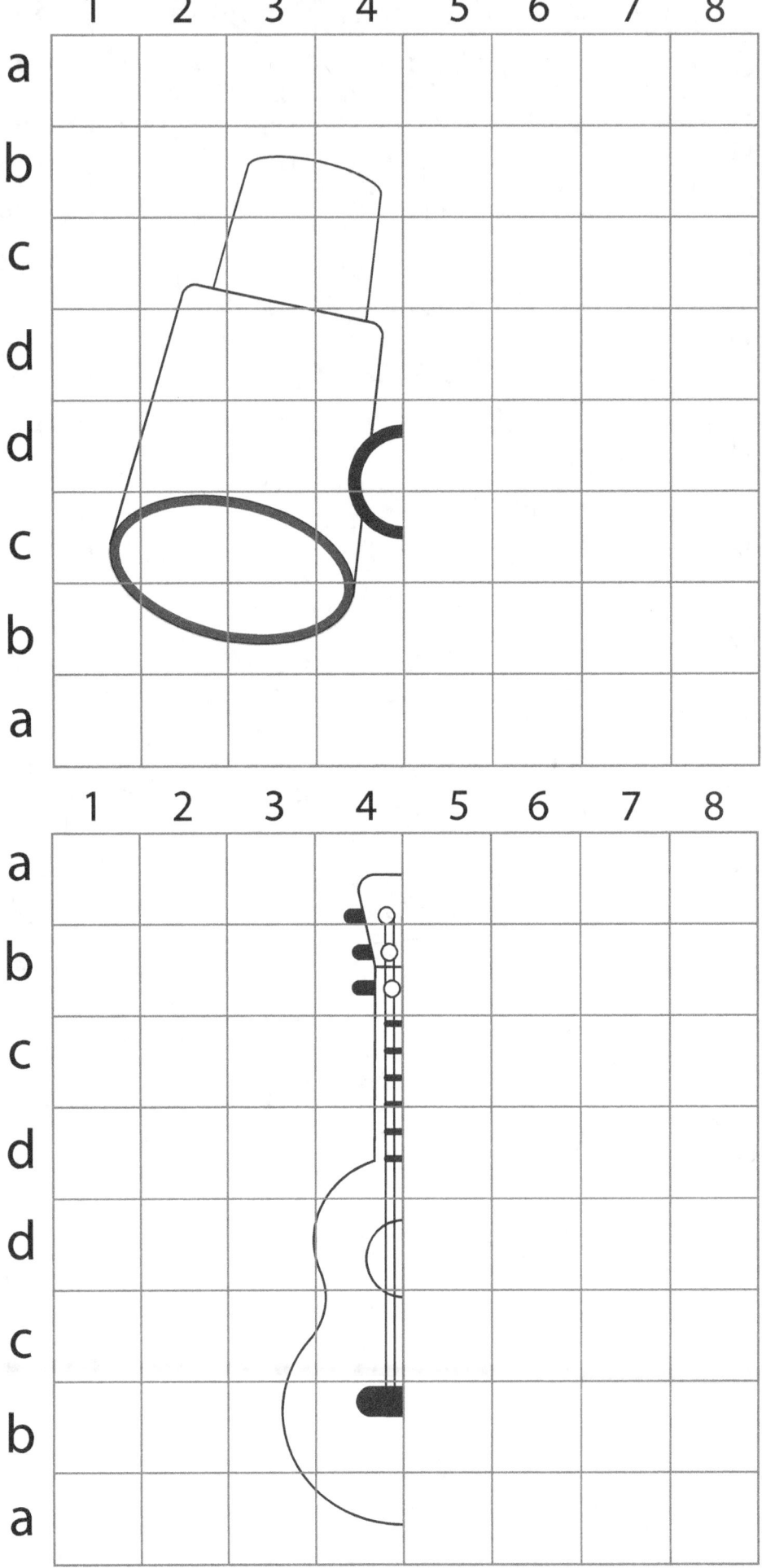

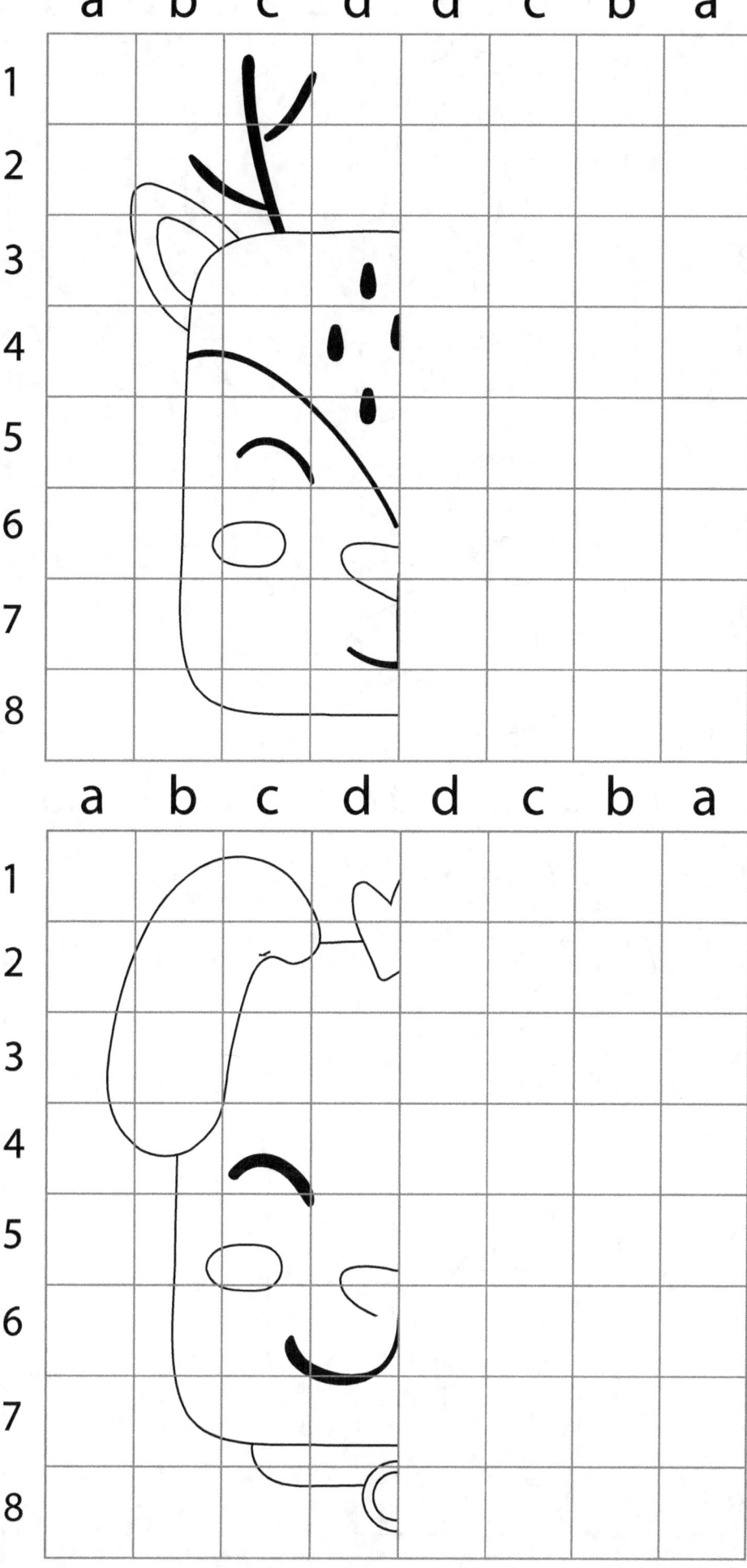

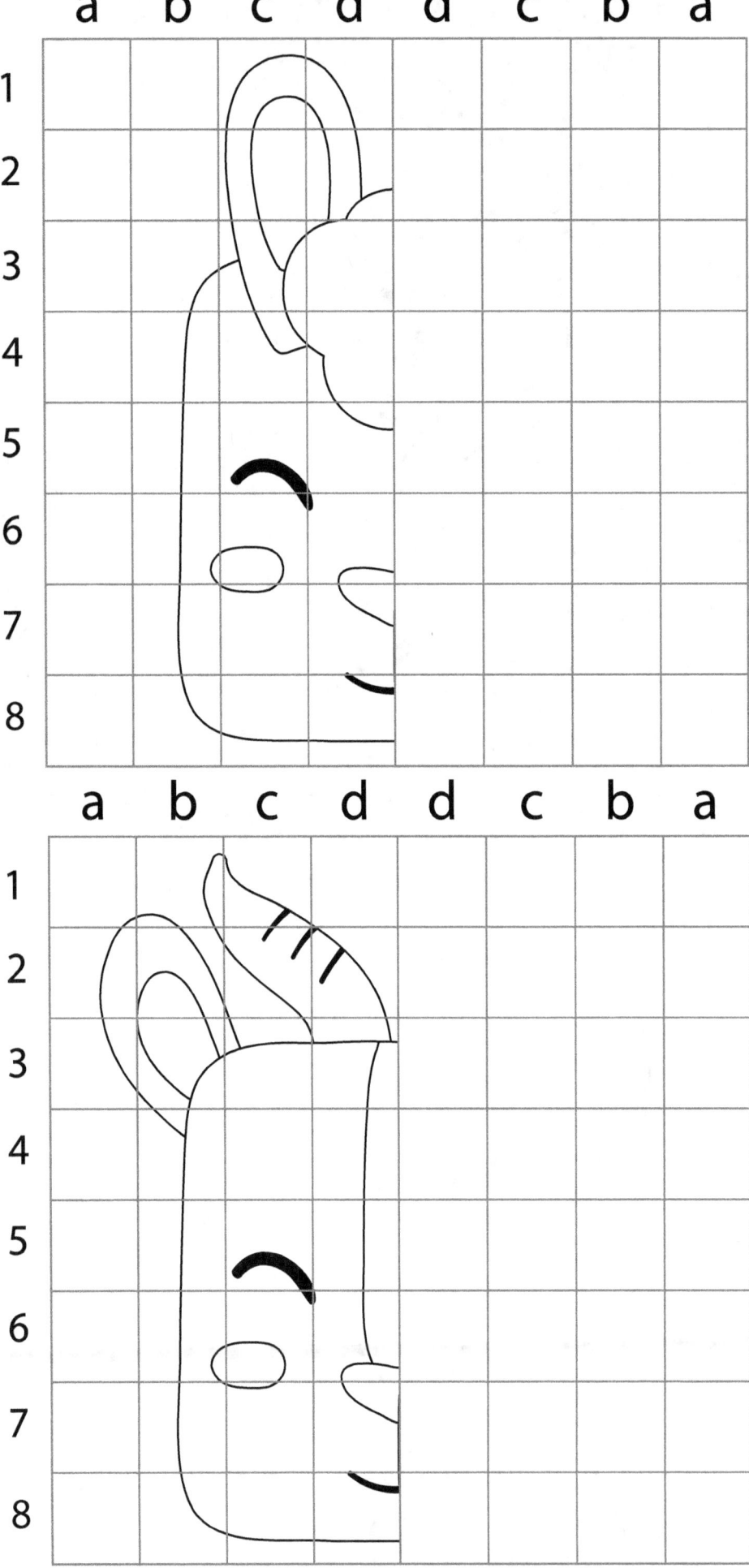

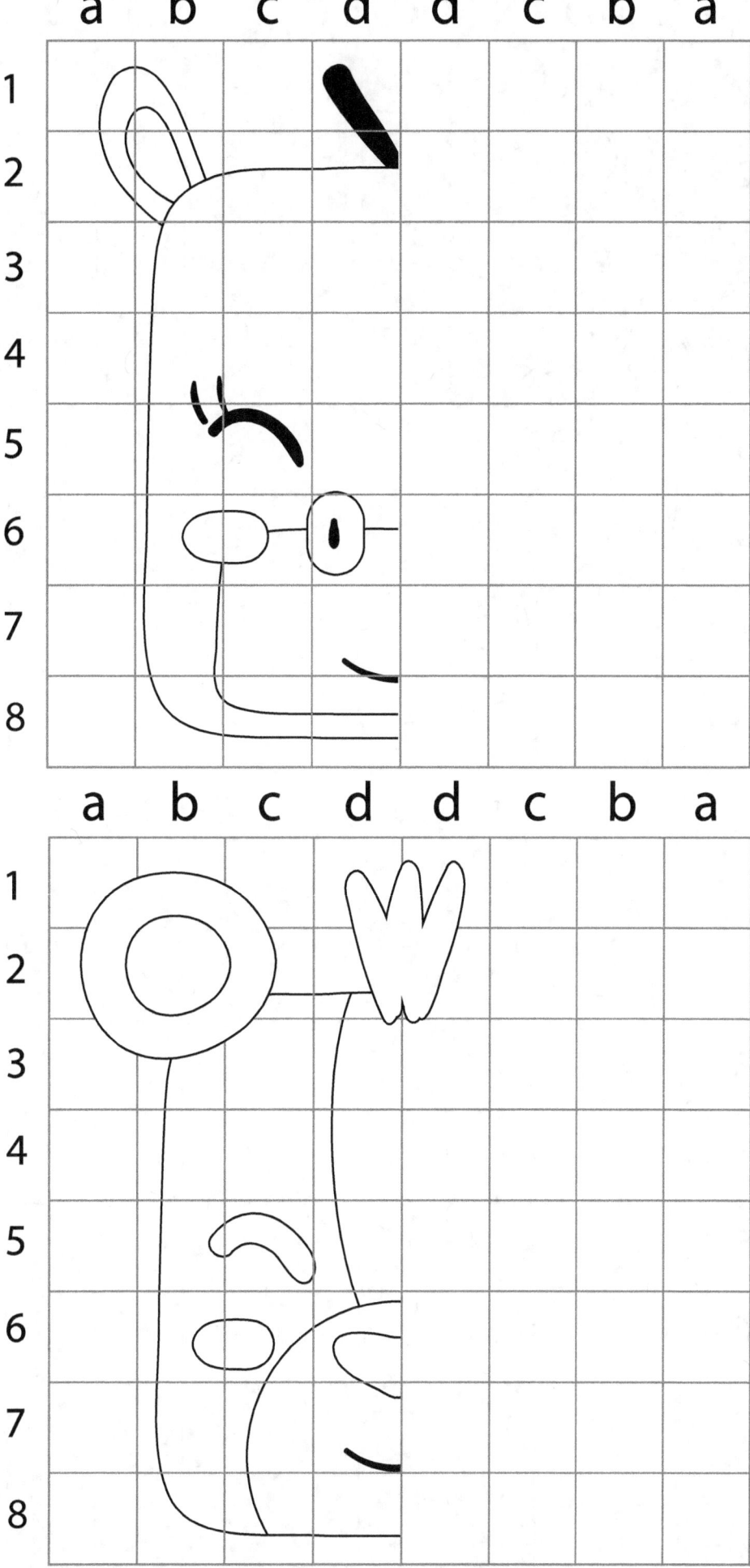

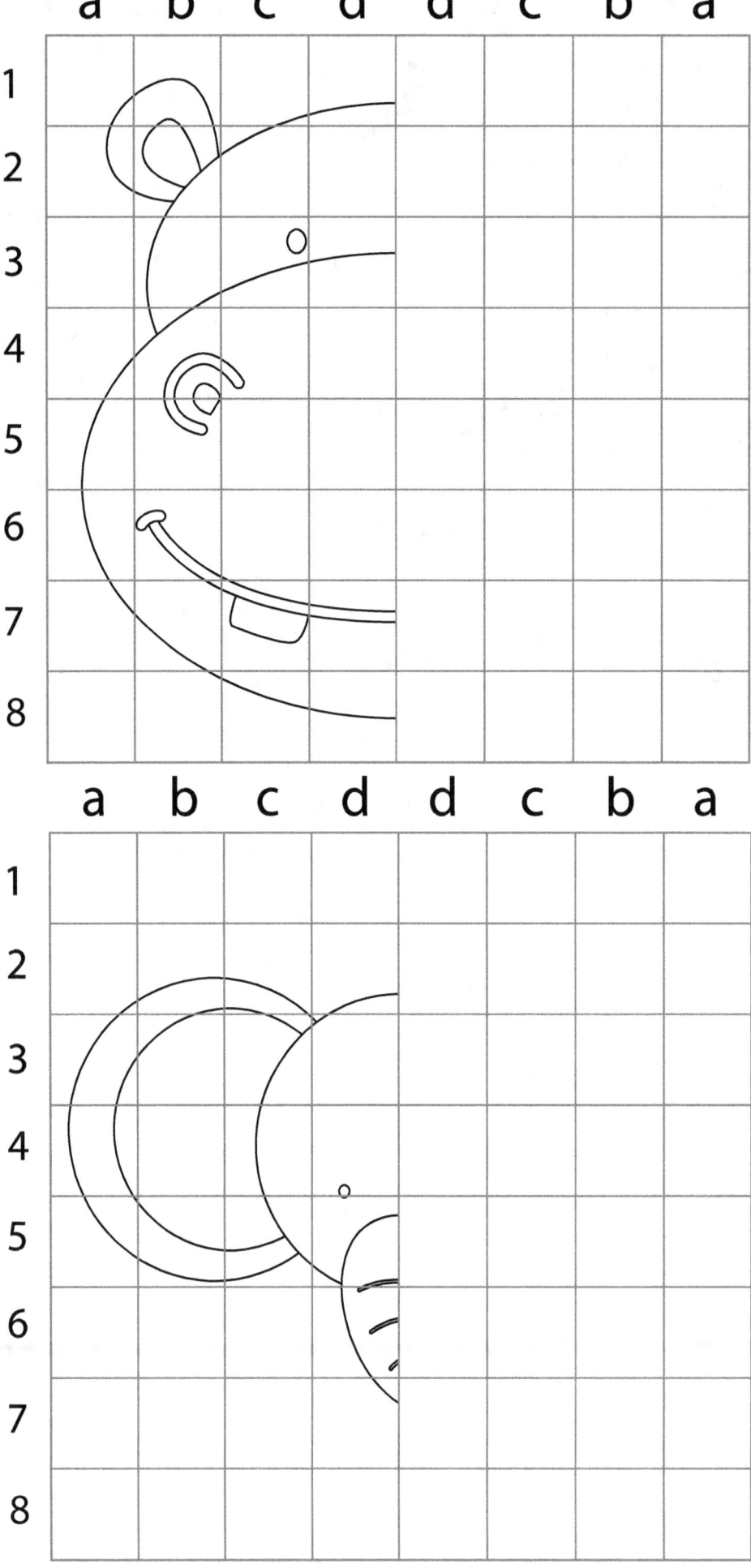

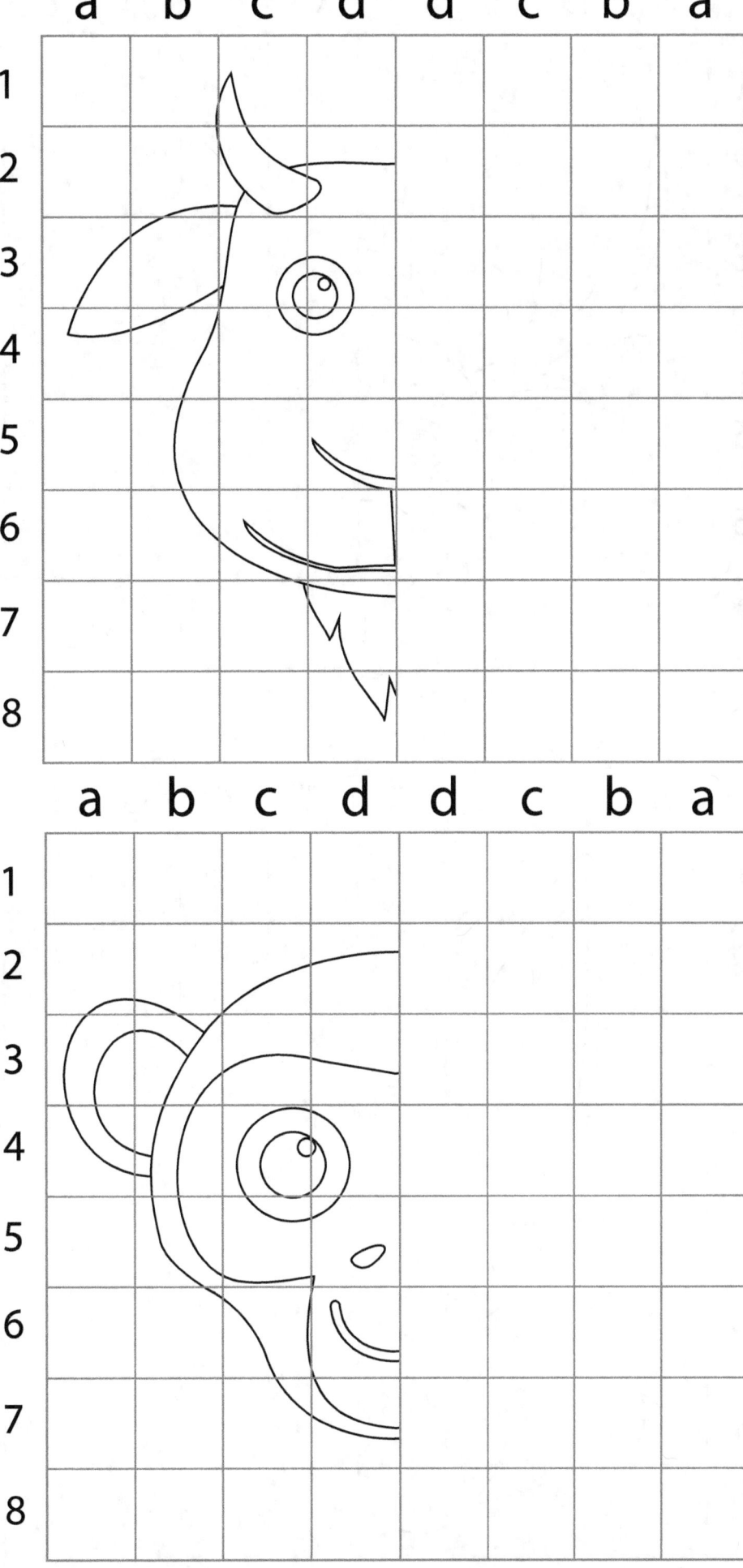

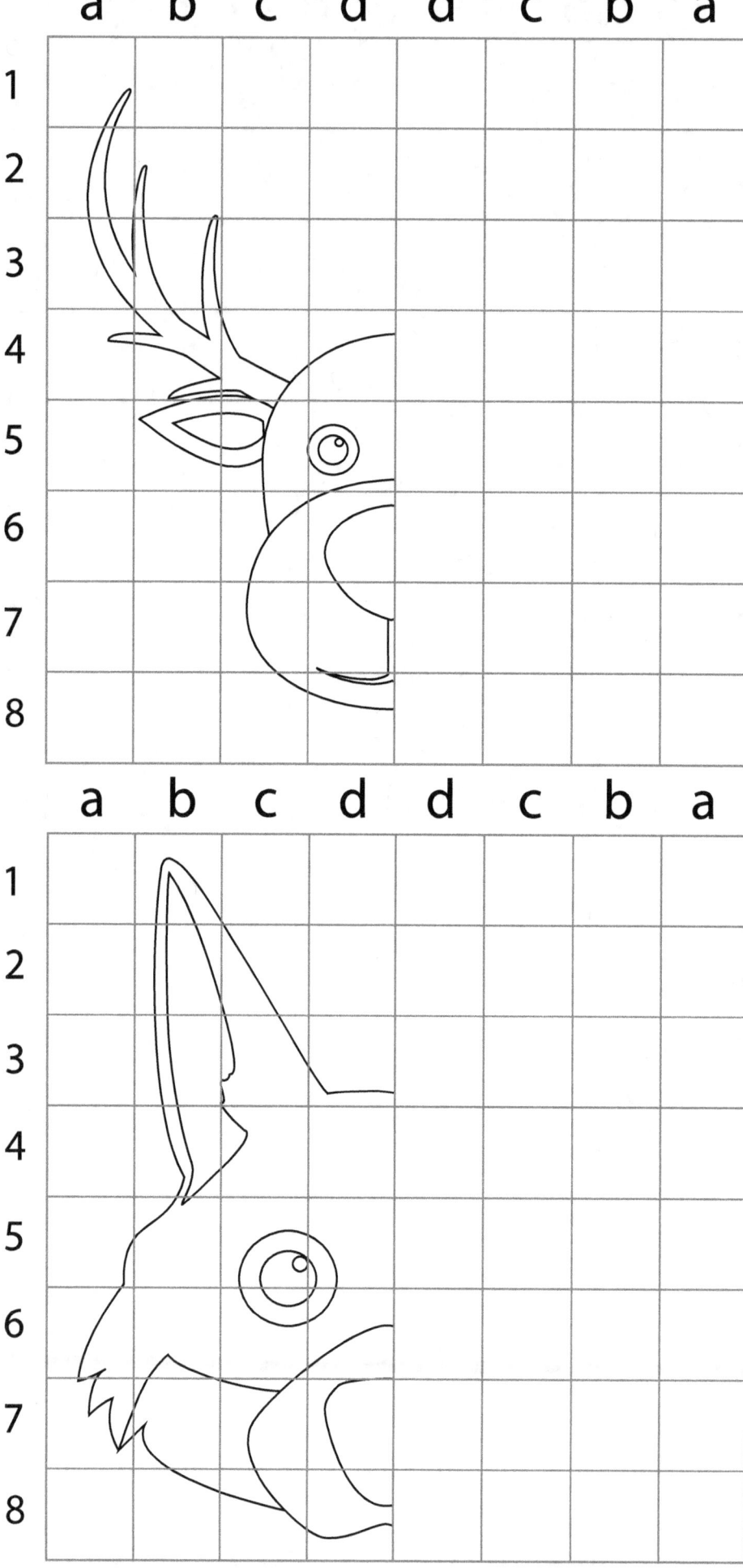

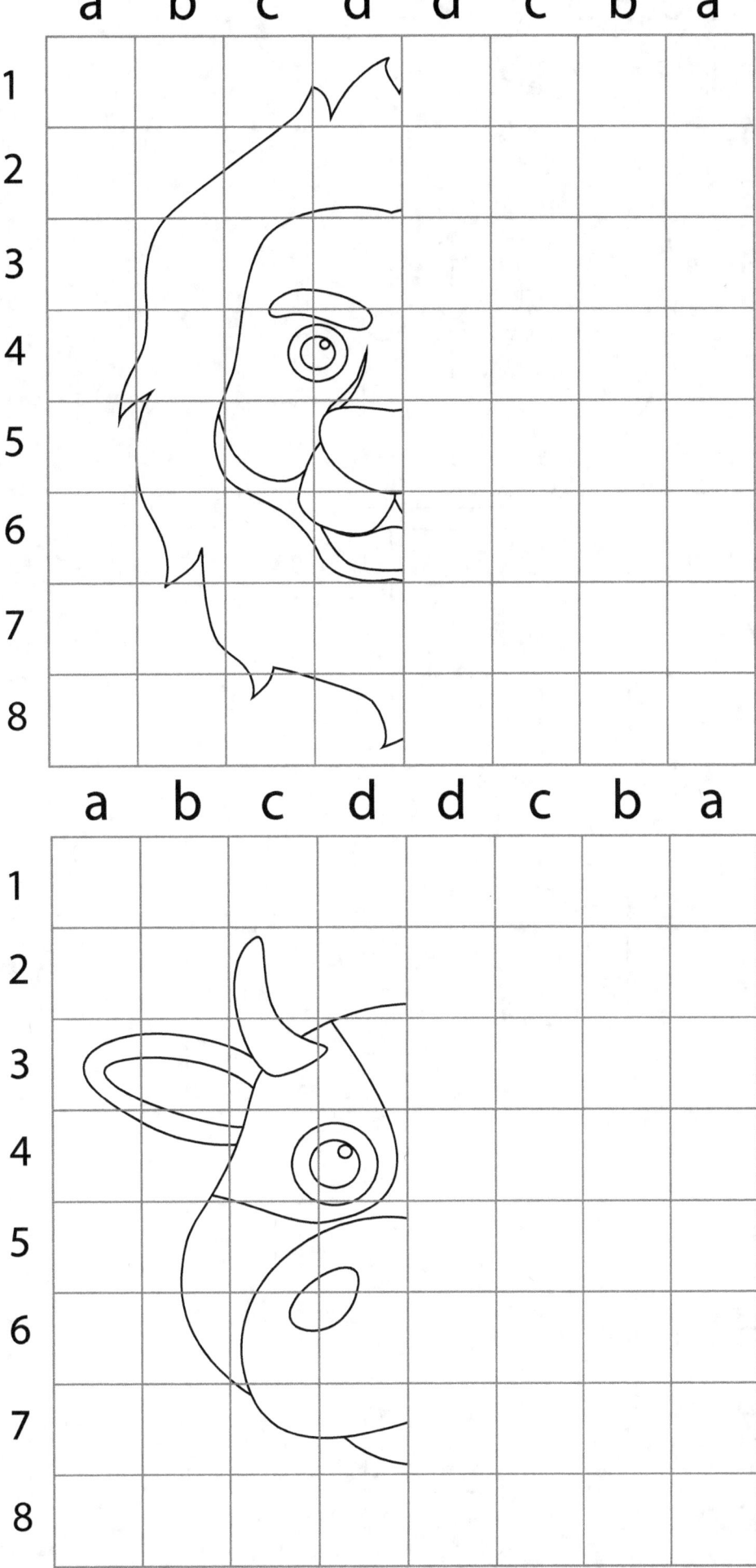

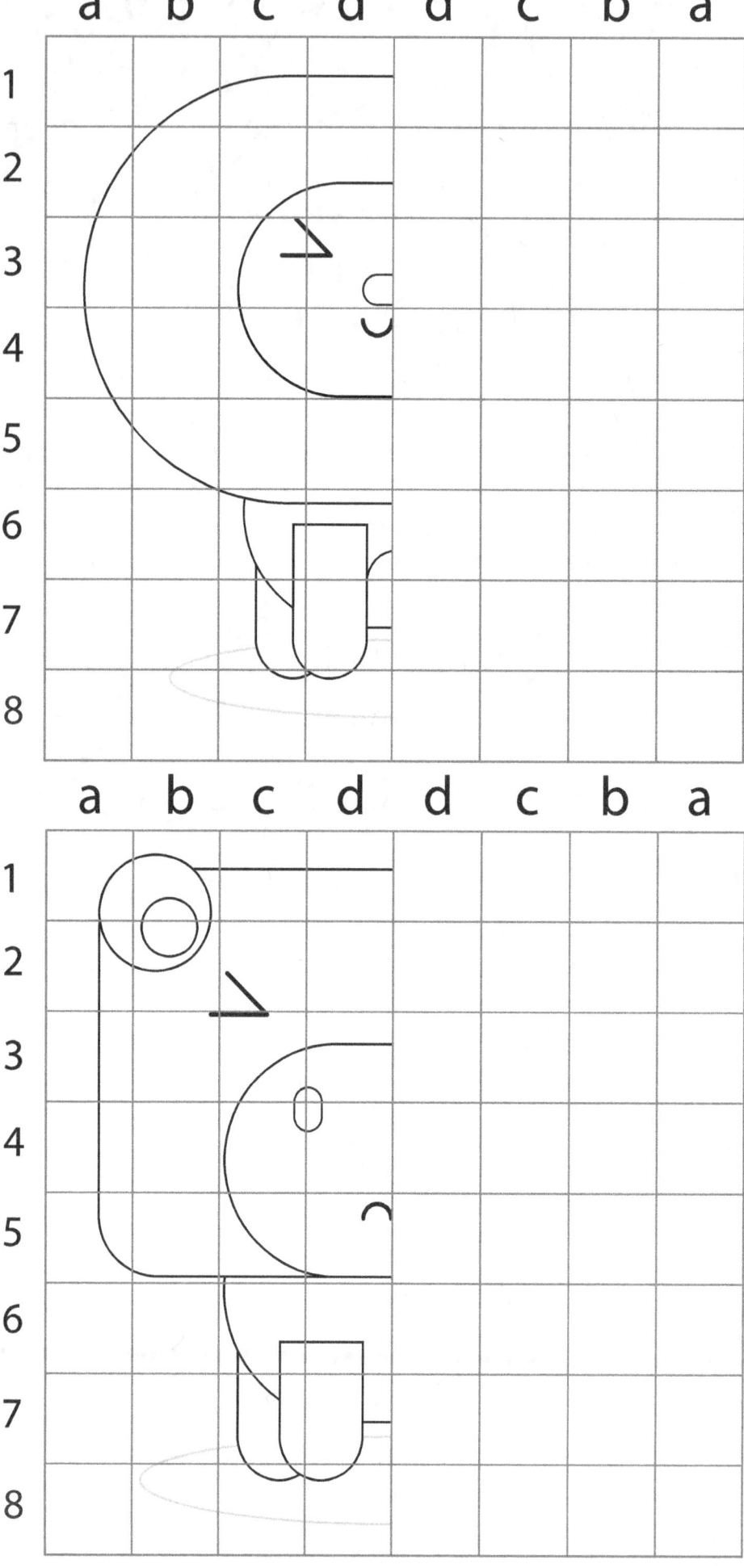

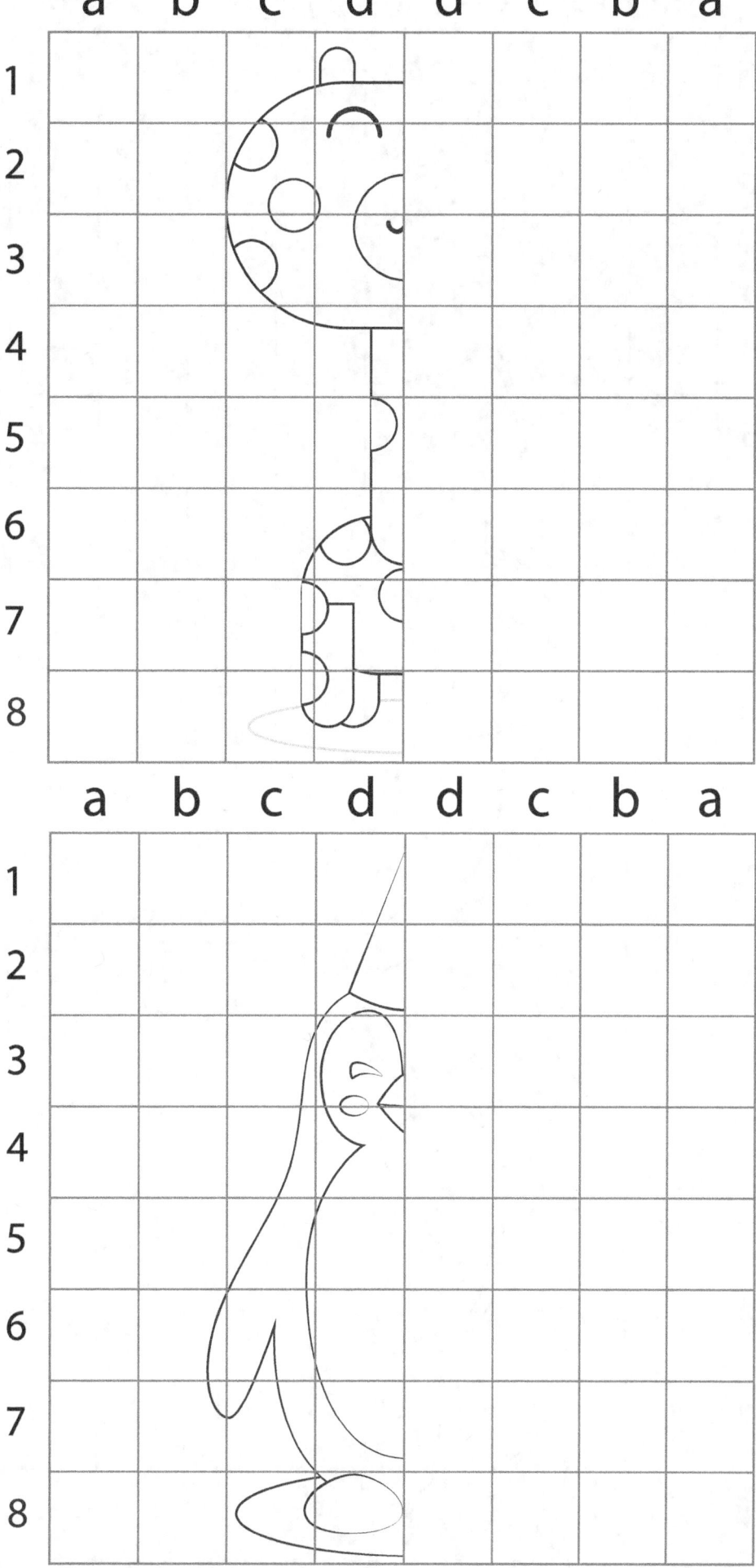

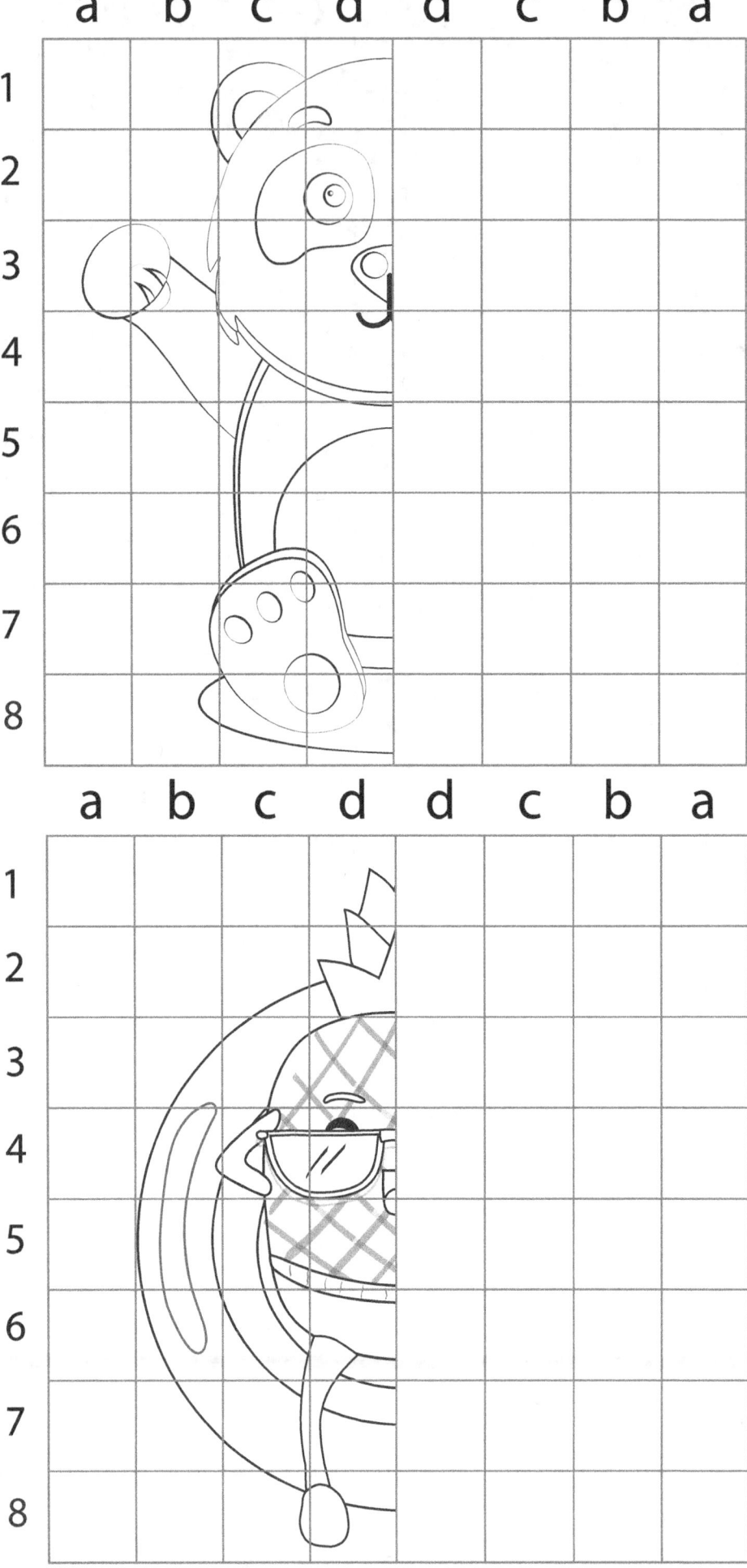

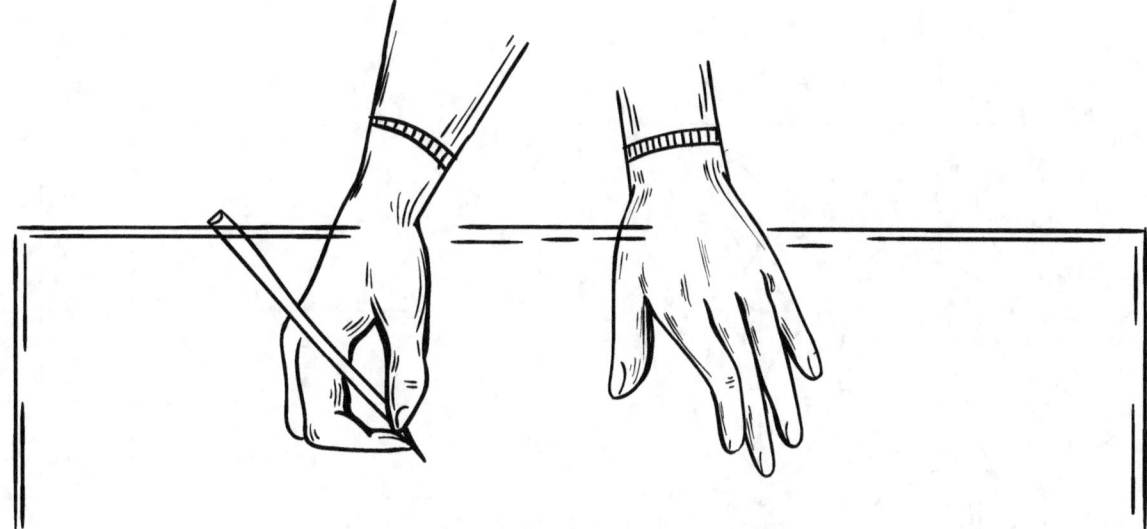

Drawing tutorial
Copy the picture using grid lines.

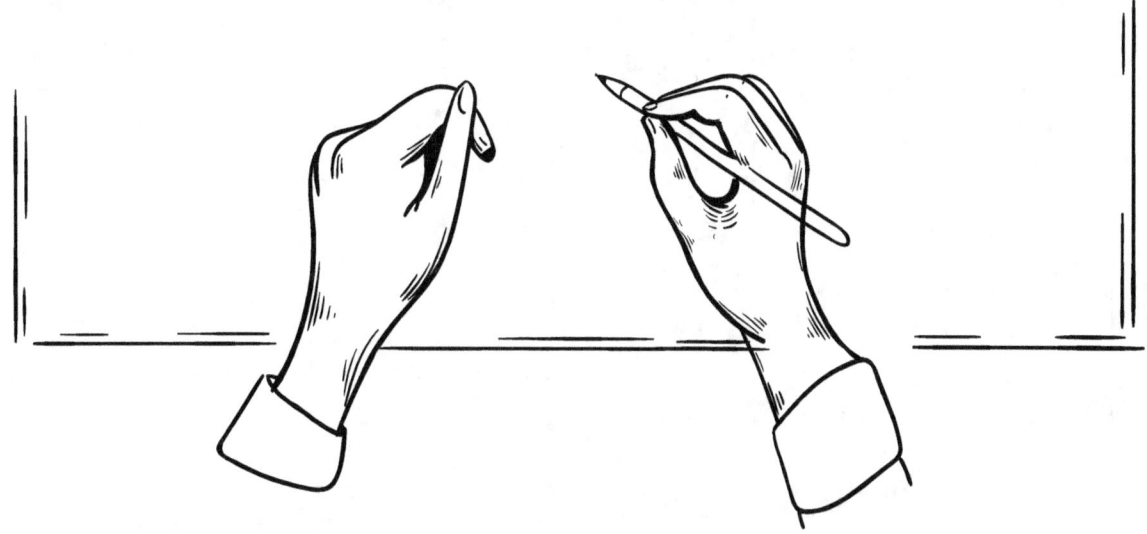

COPY THE UNICORN

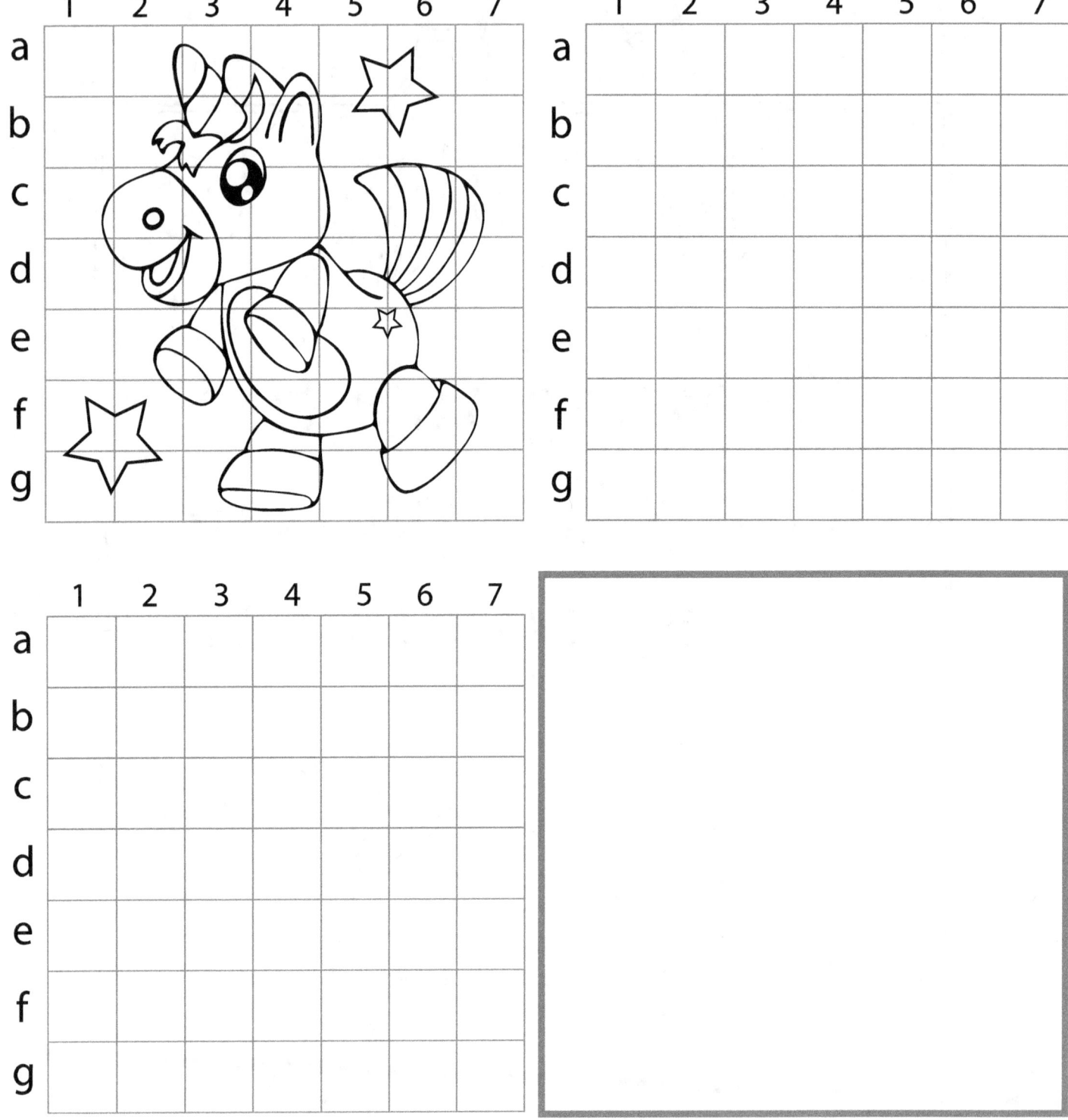

COPY THE ELEPHANT

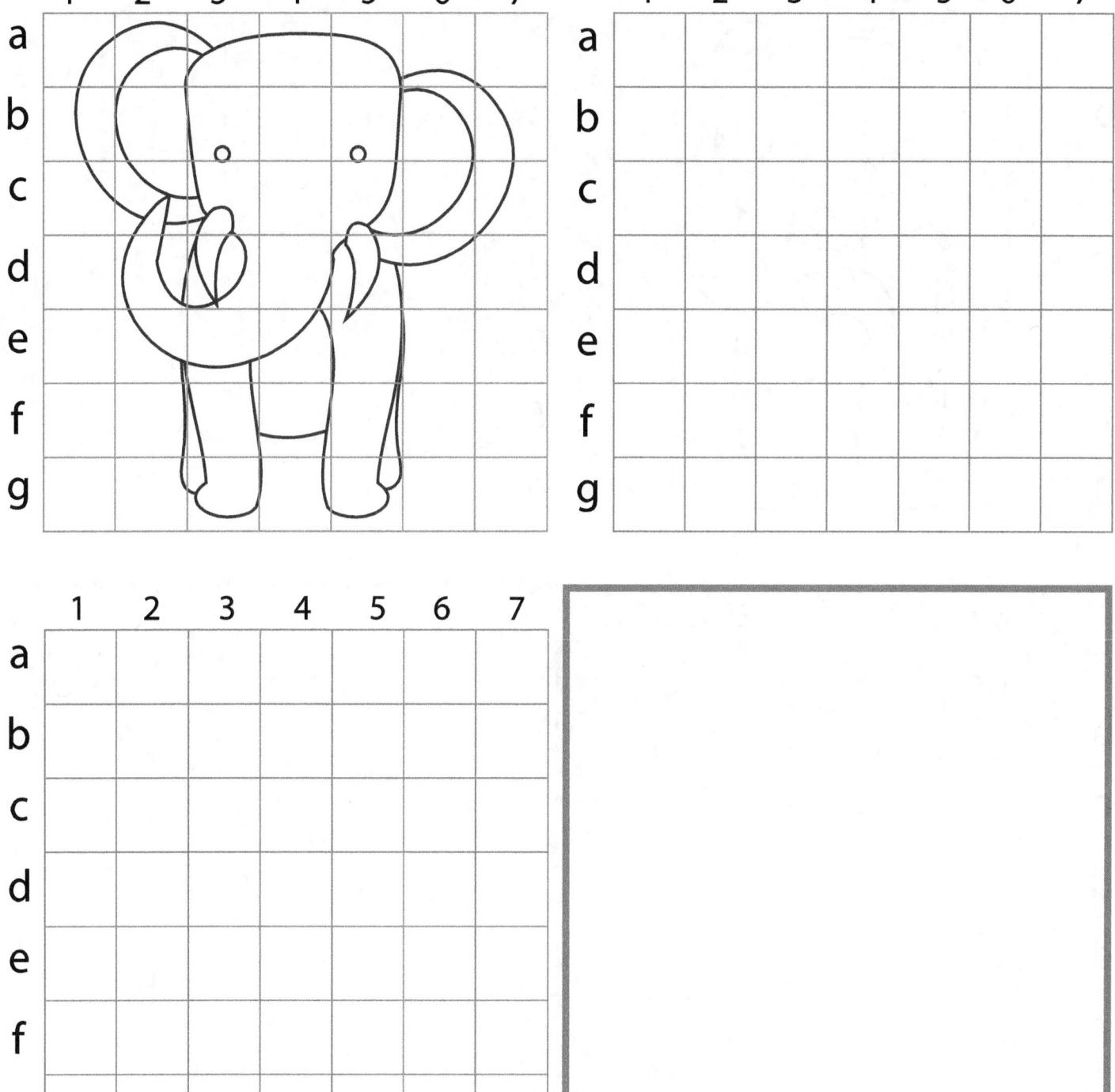

COPY THE BEAR

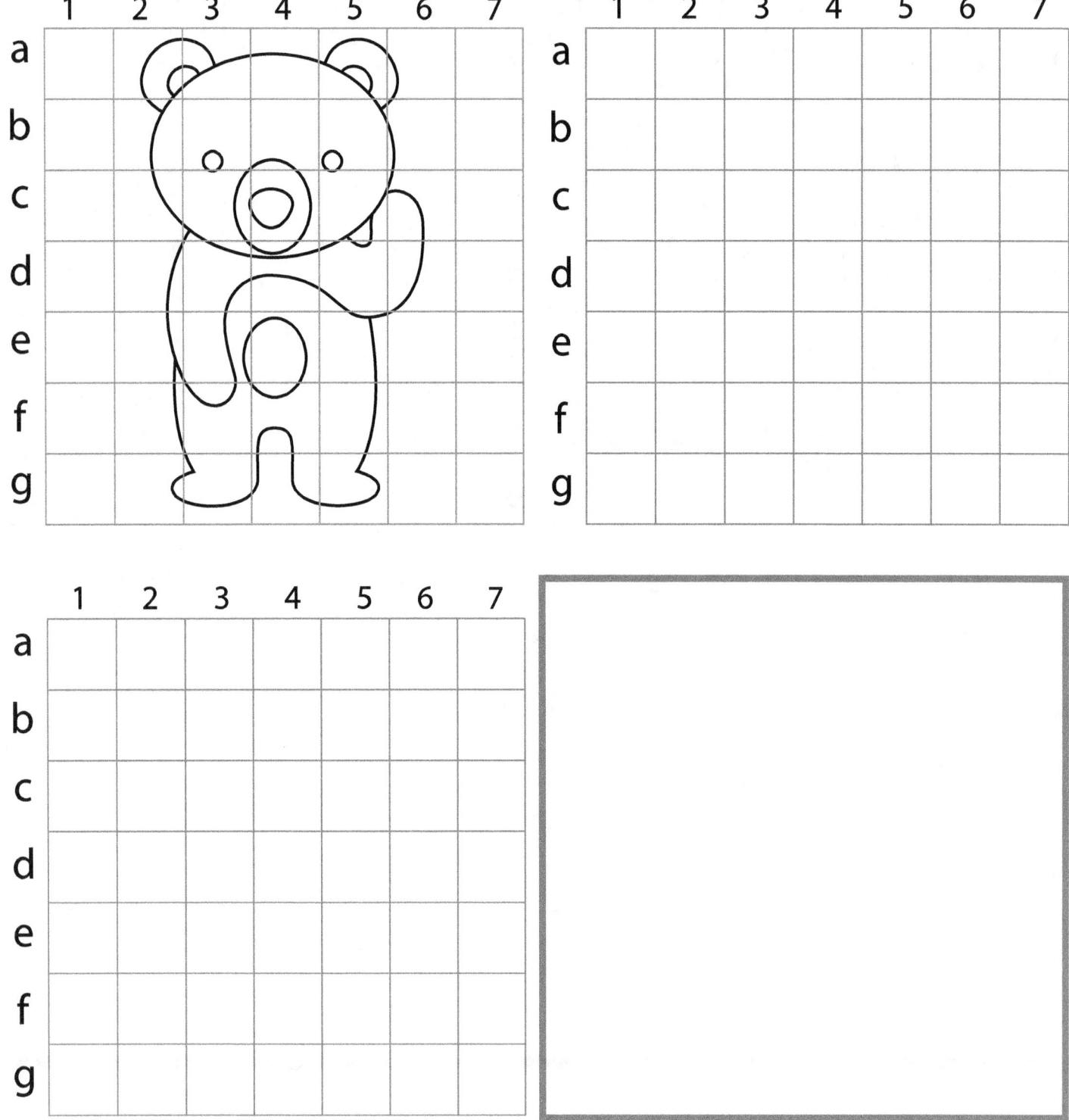

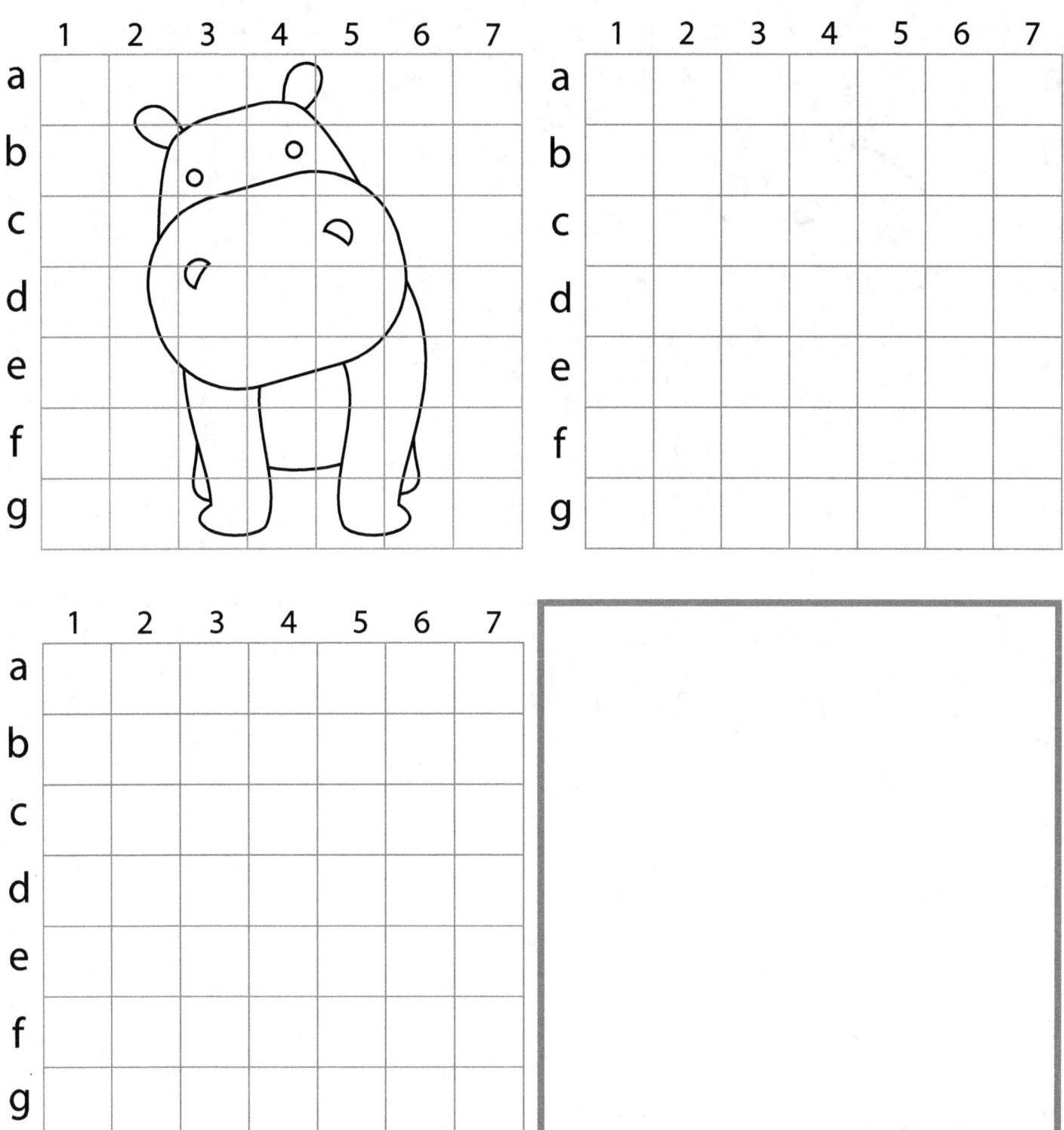

COPY THE GIRAFFE

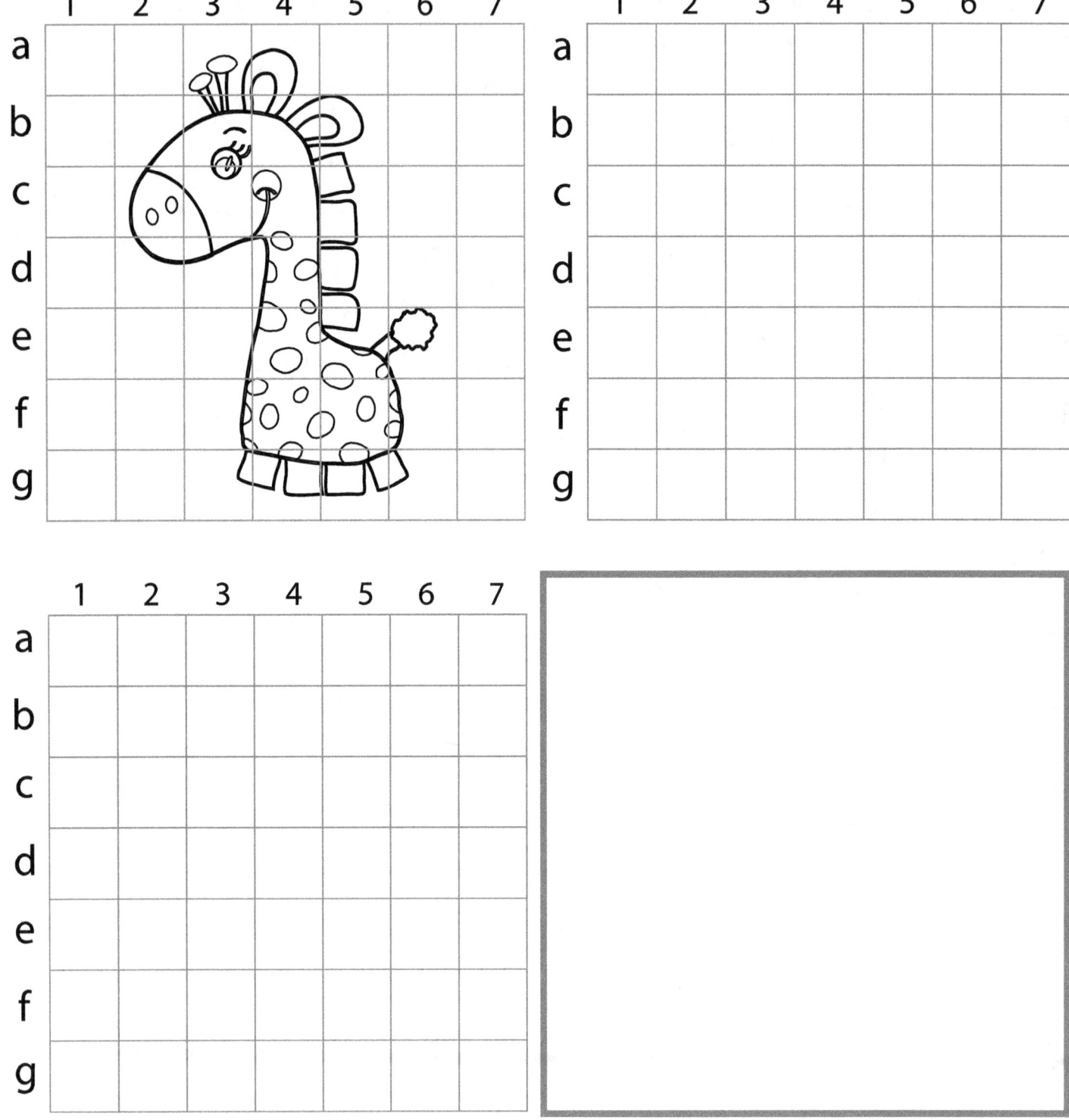

COPY THE ZEBRA

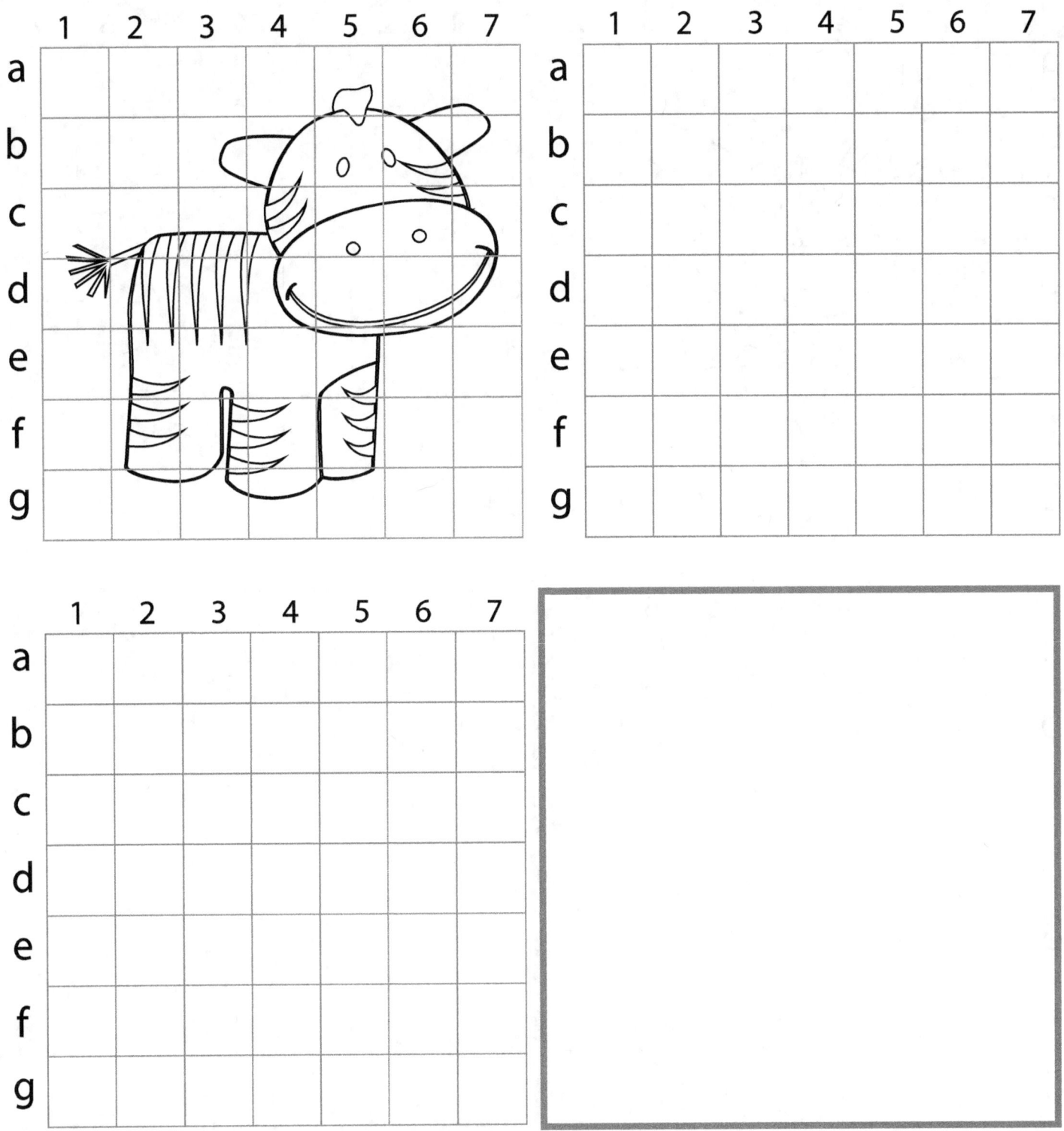

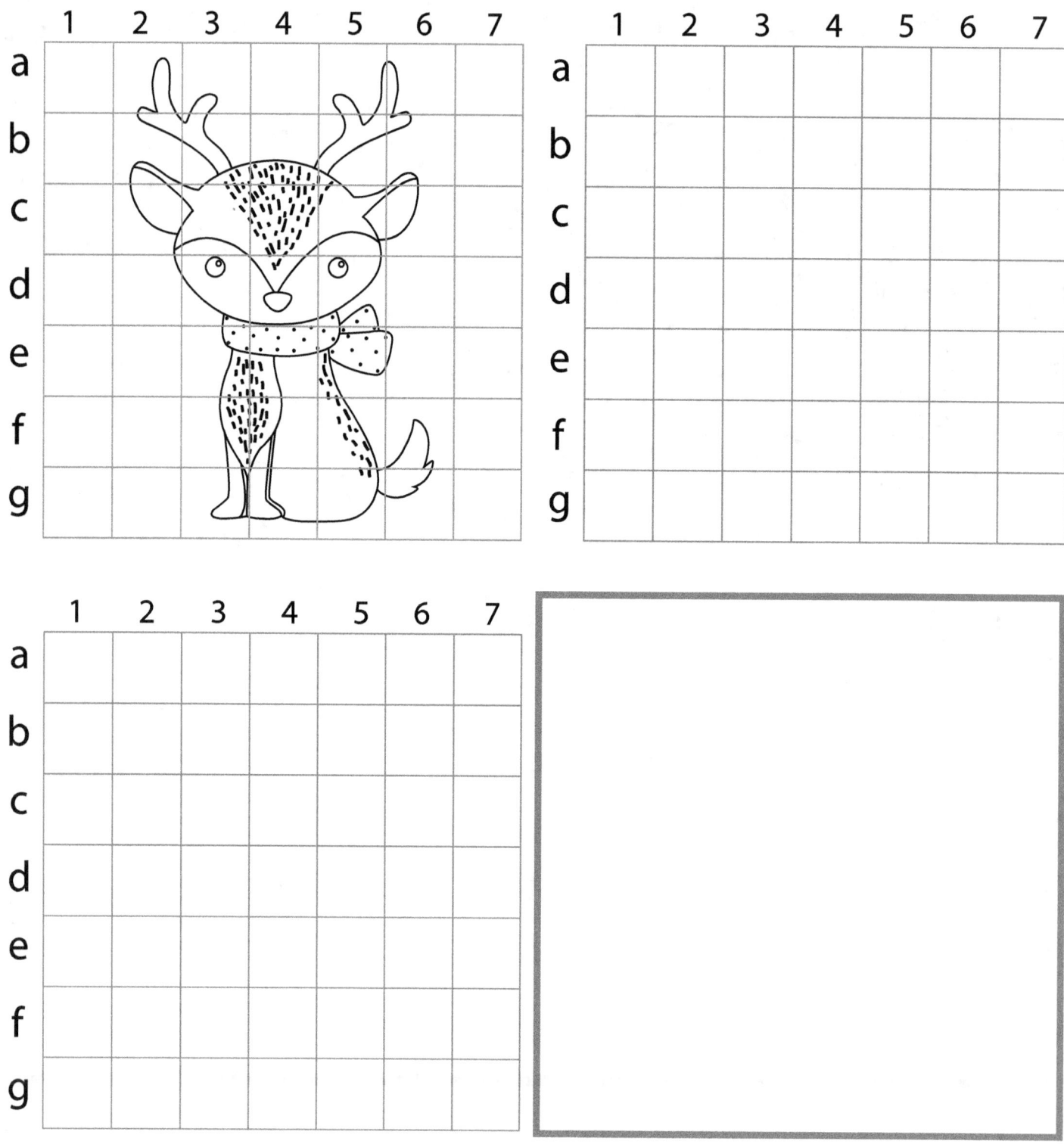

COPY THE RACCOON

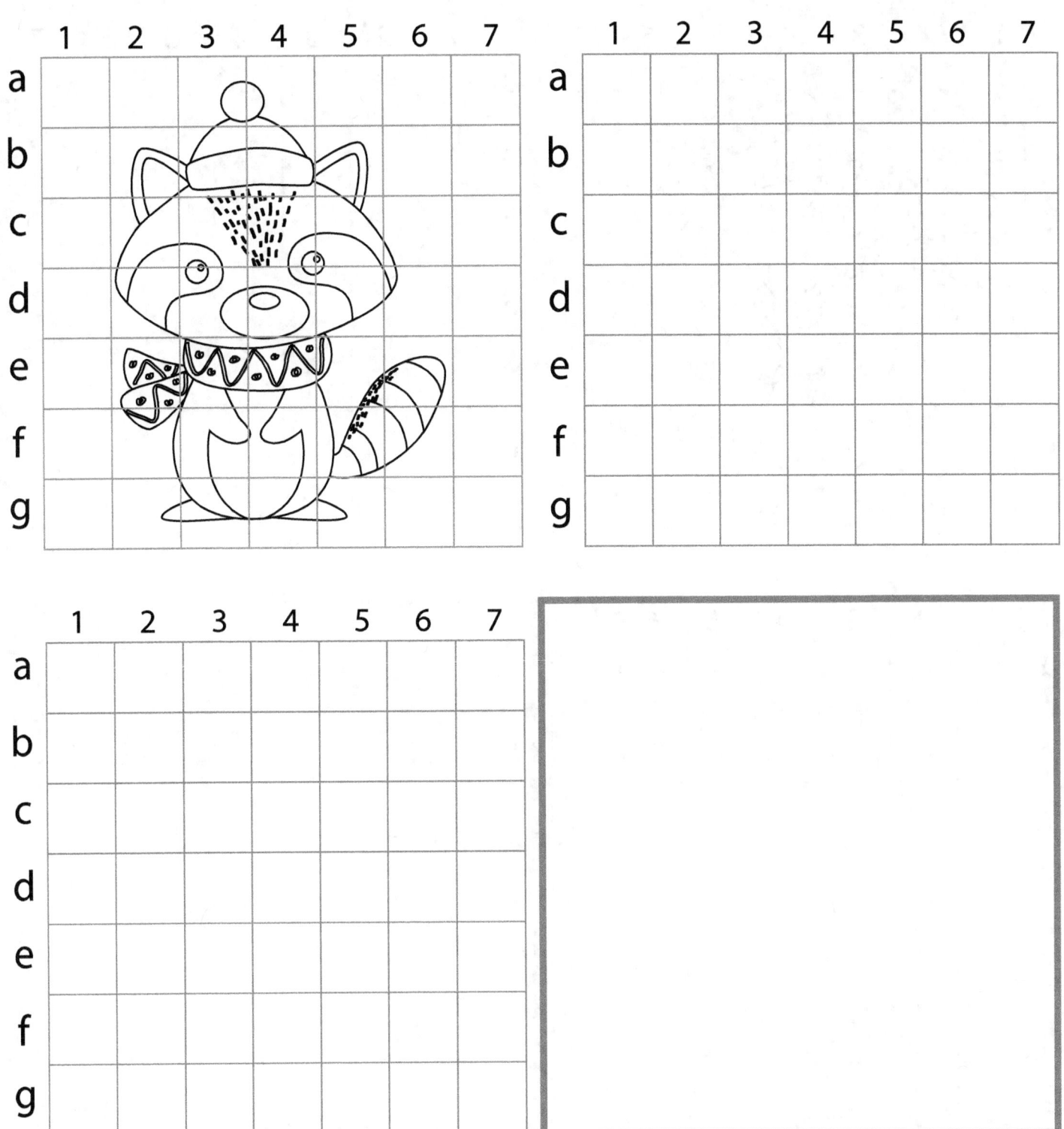

COPY THE FOX

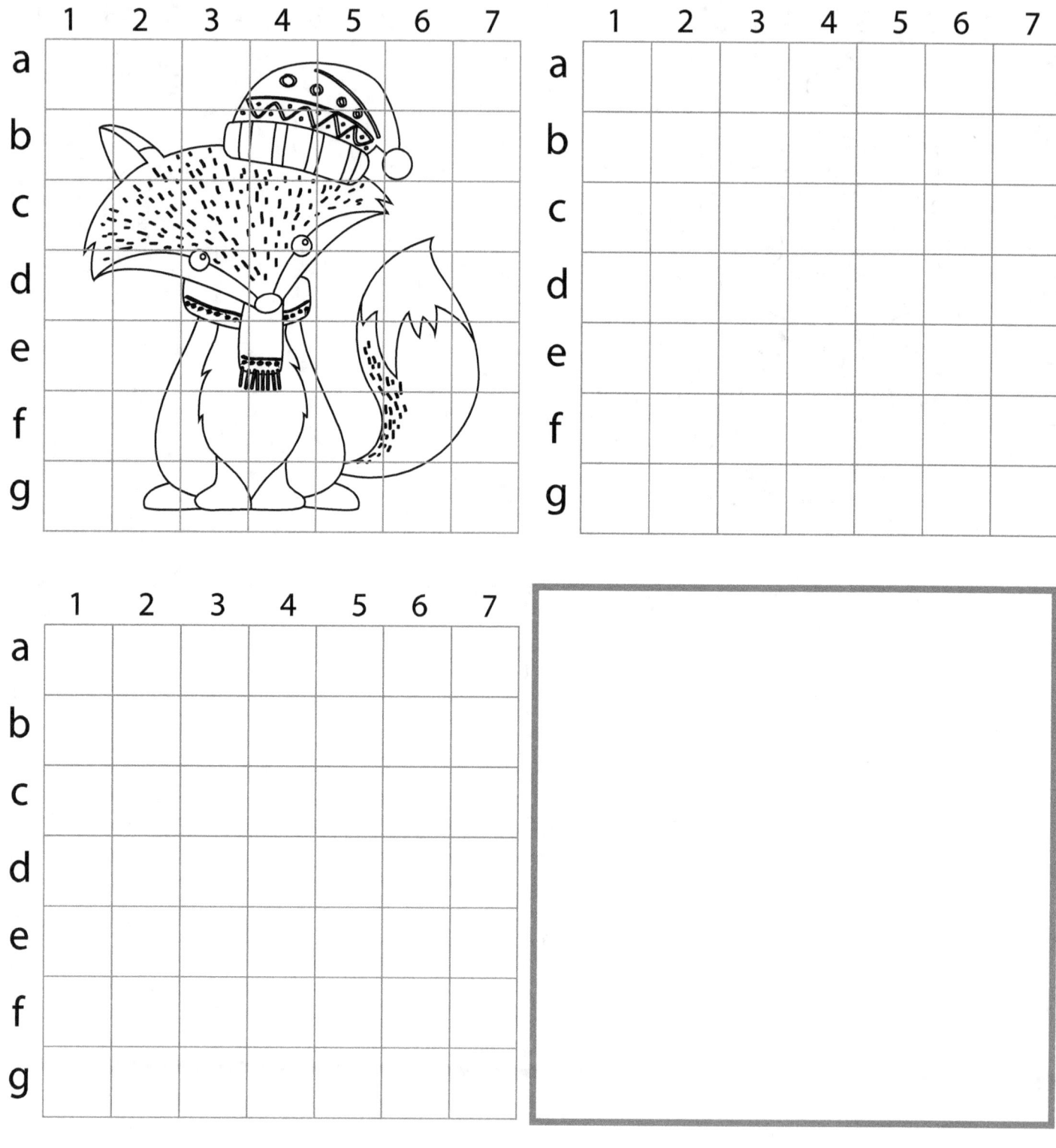

COPY THE RABBIT

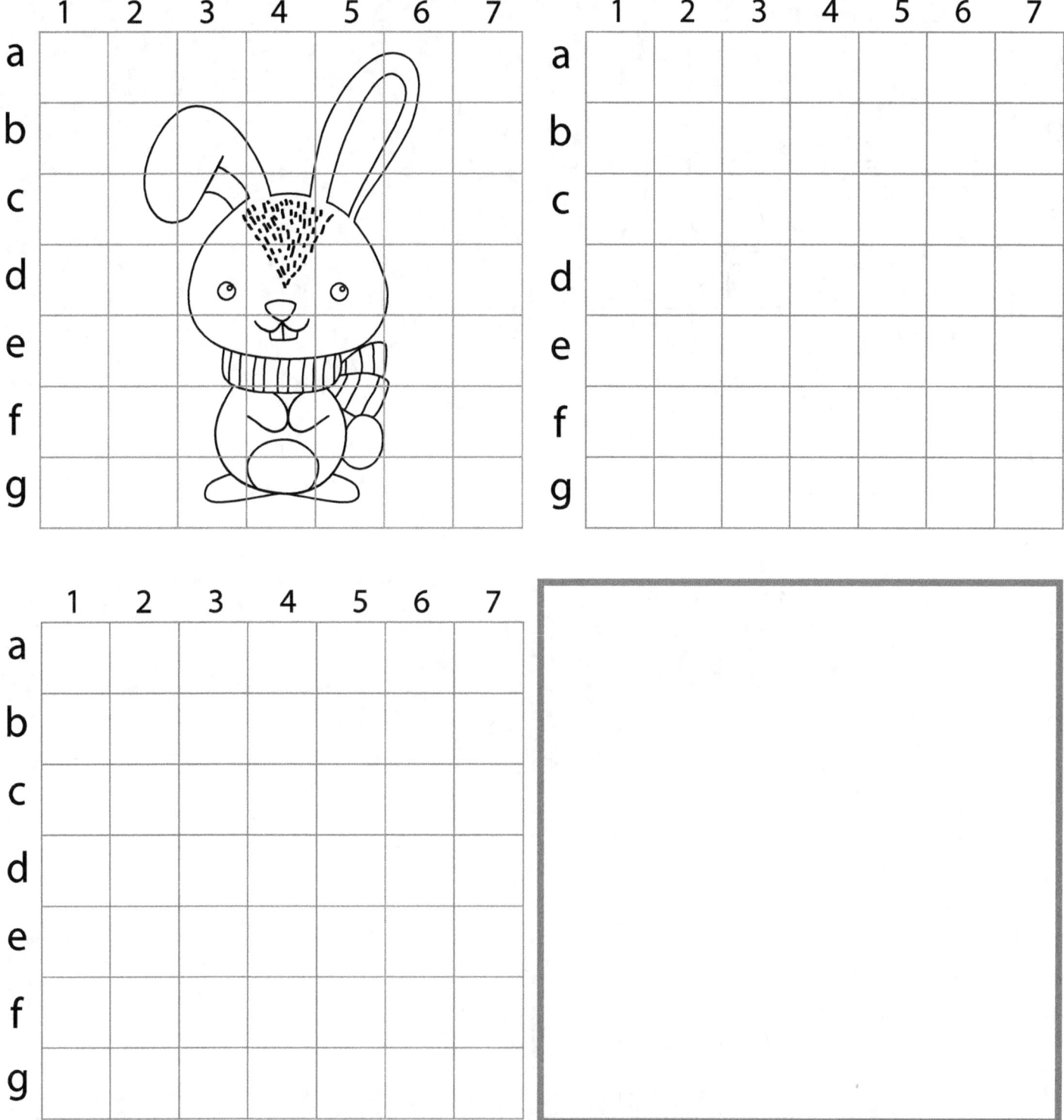

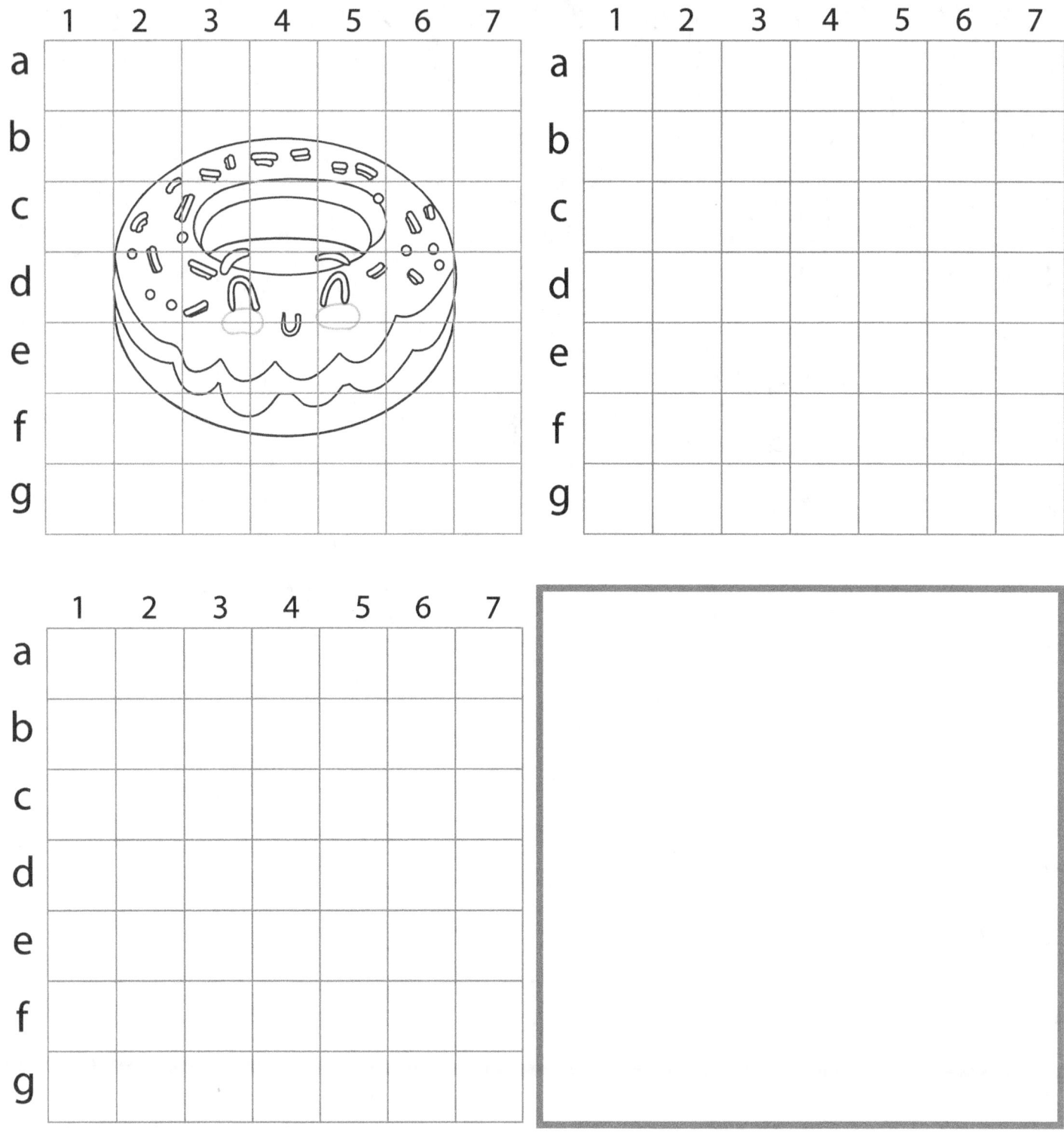

COPY THE ICE CREAM

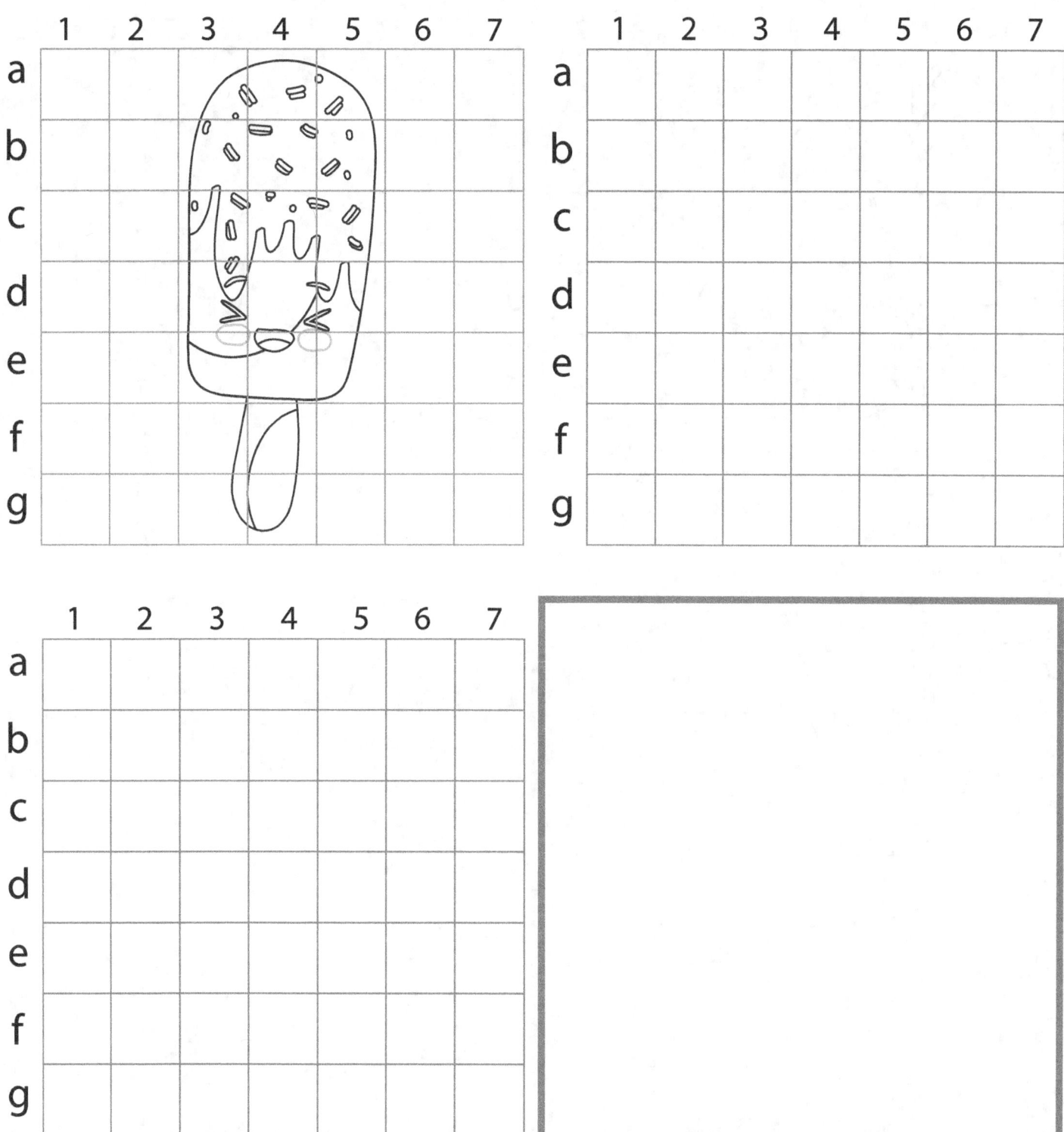

COPY THE WATERMELON

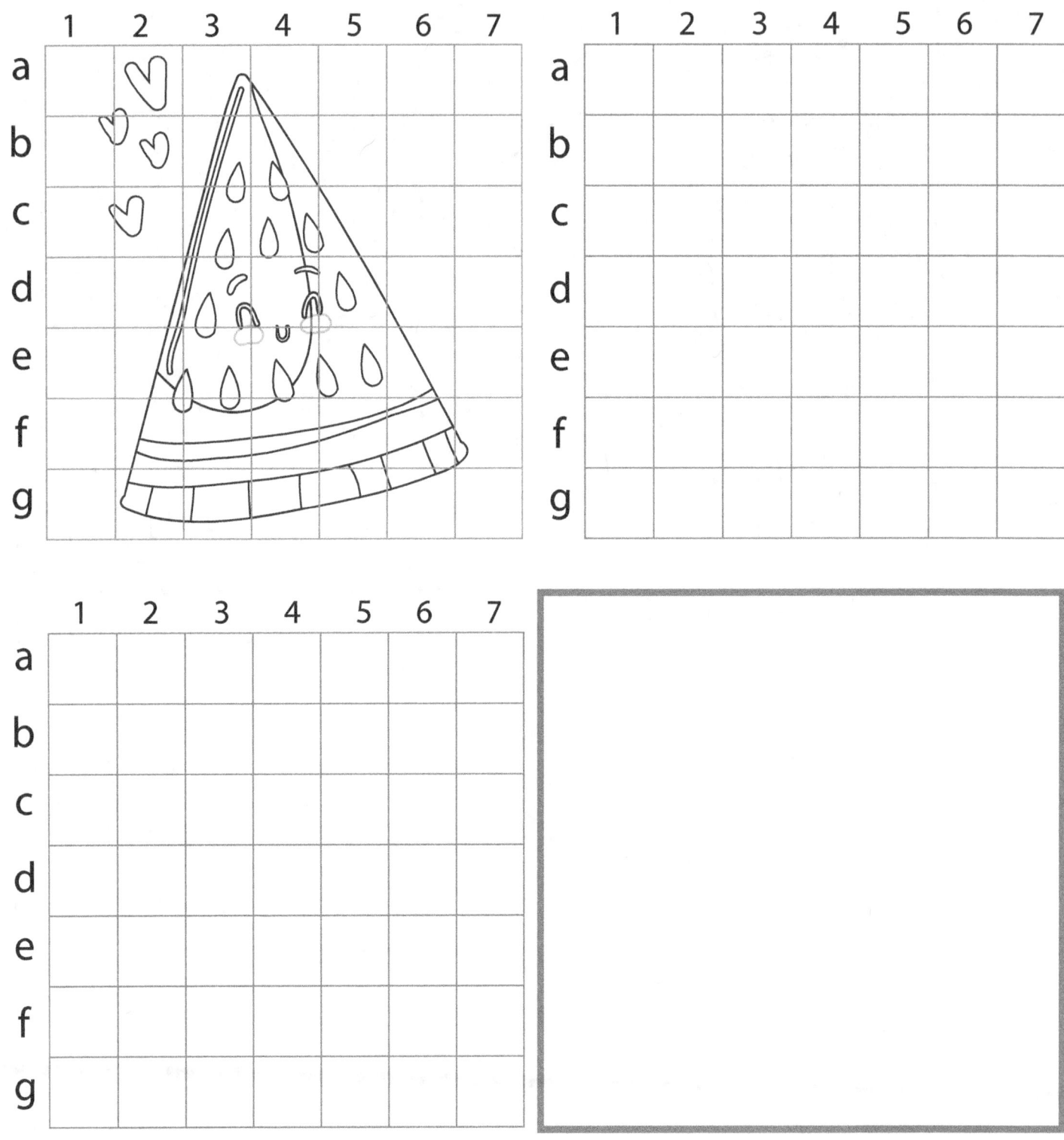

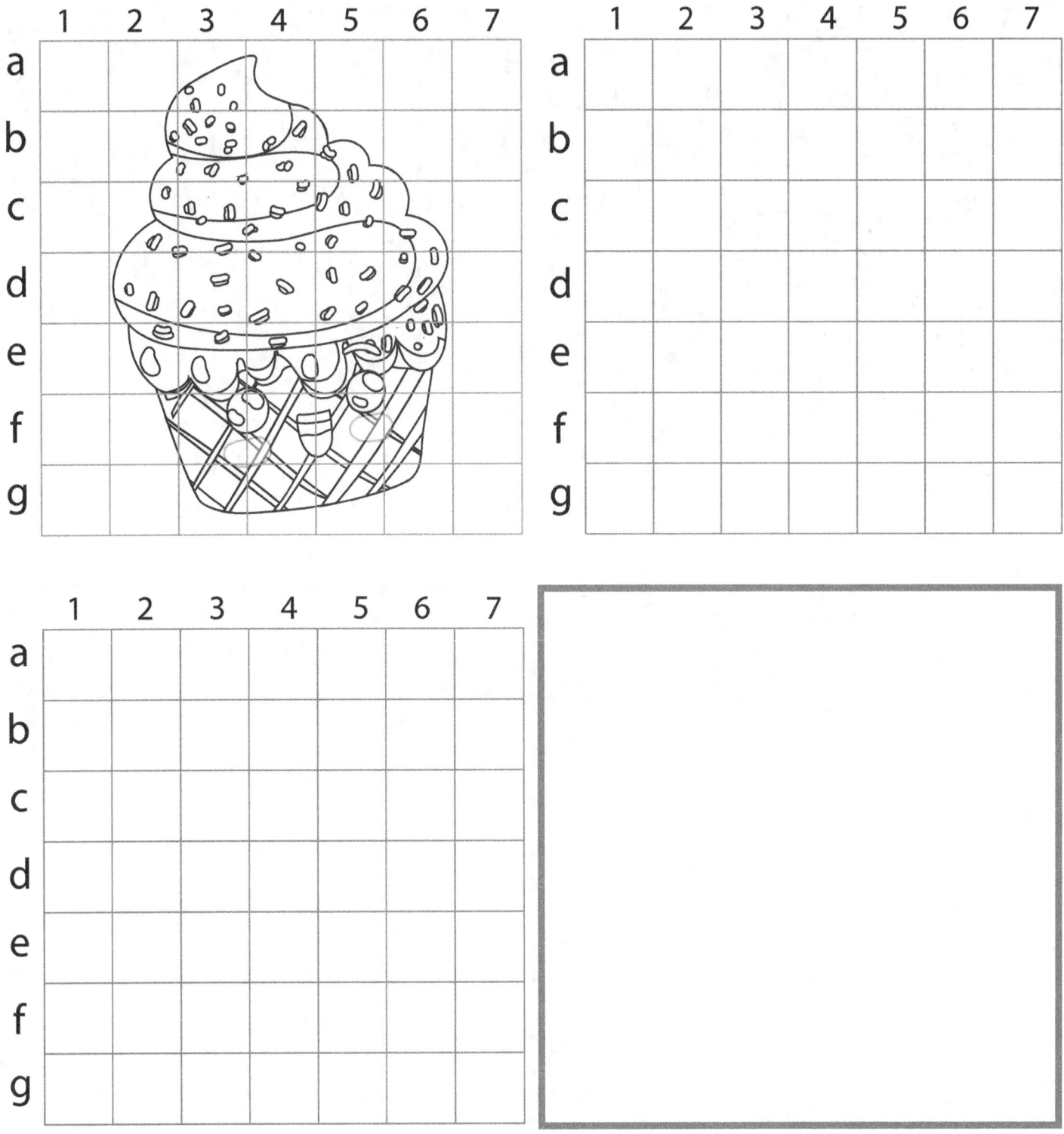

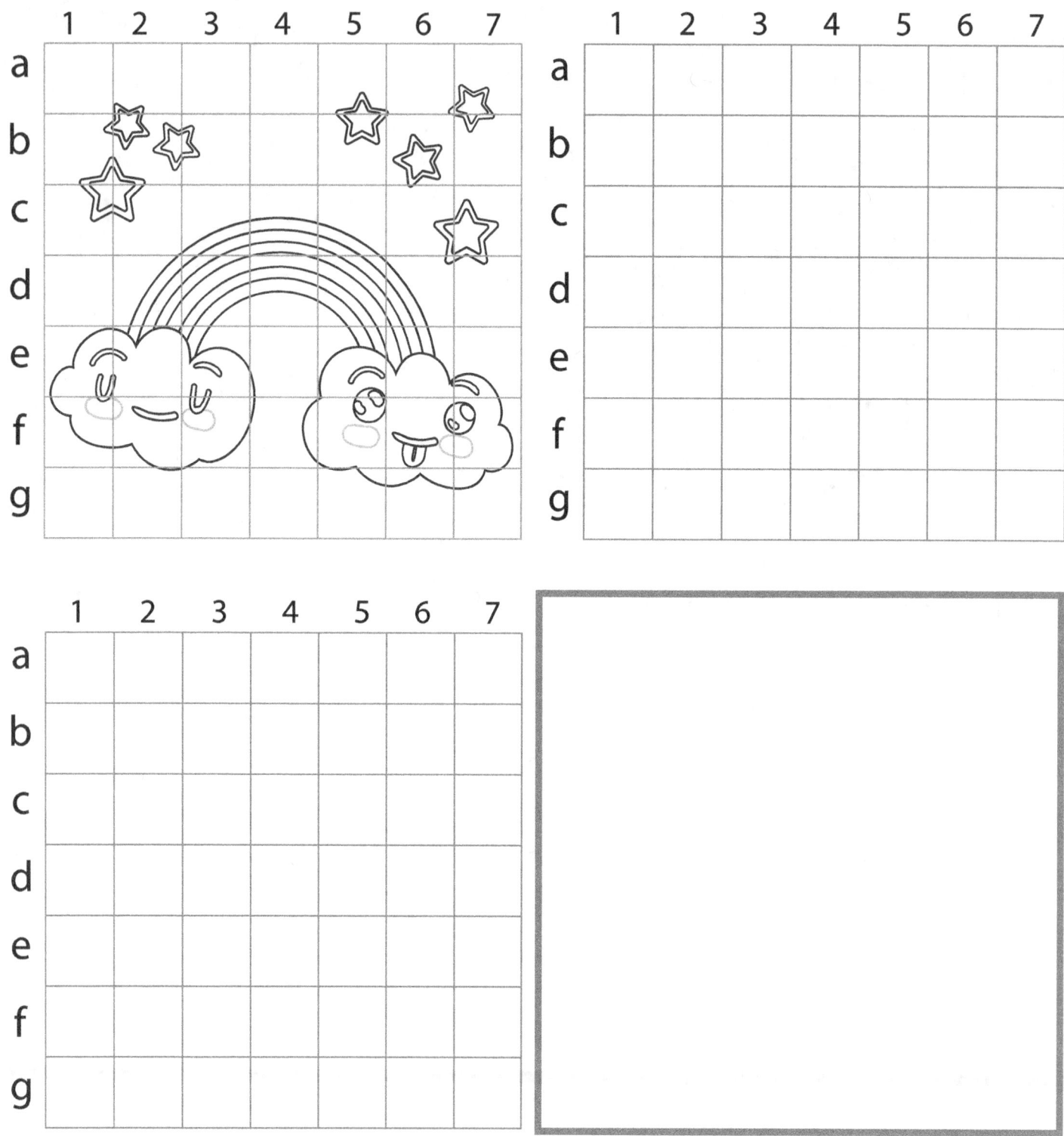

COPY THE DEER

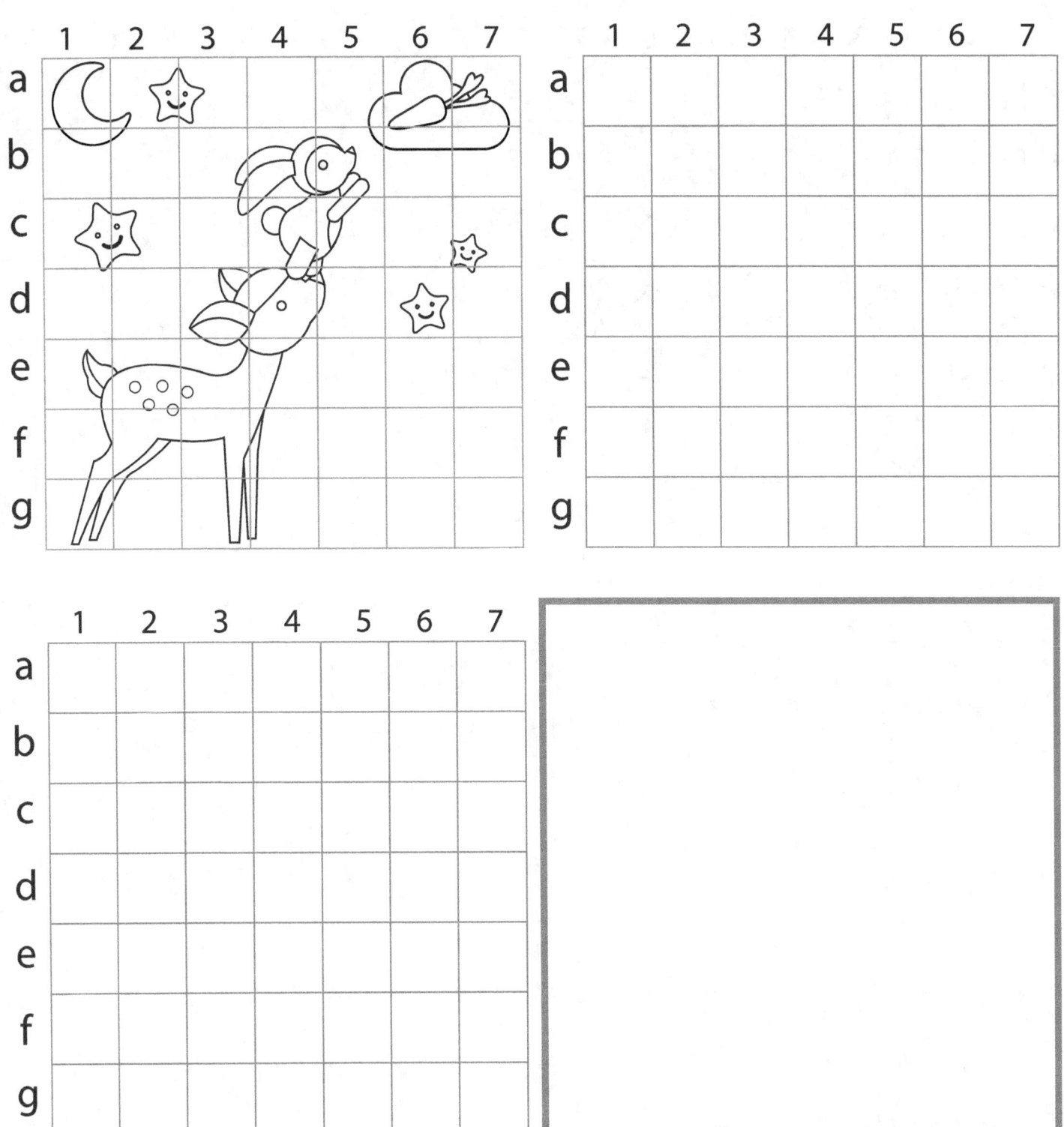

COPY THE HAPPY UNICORN

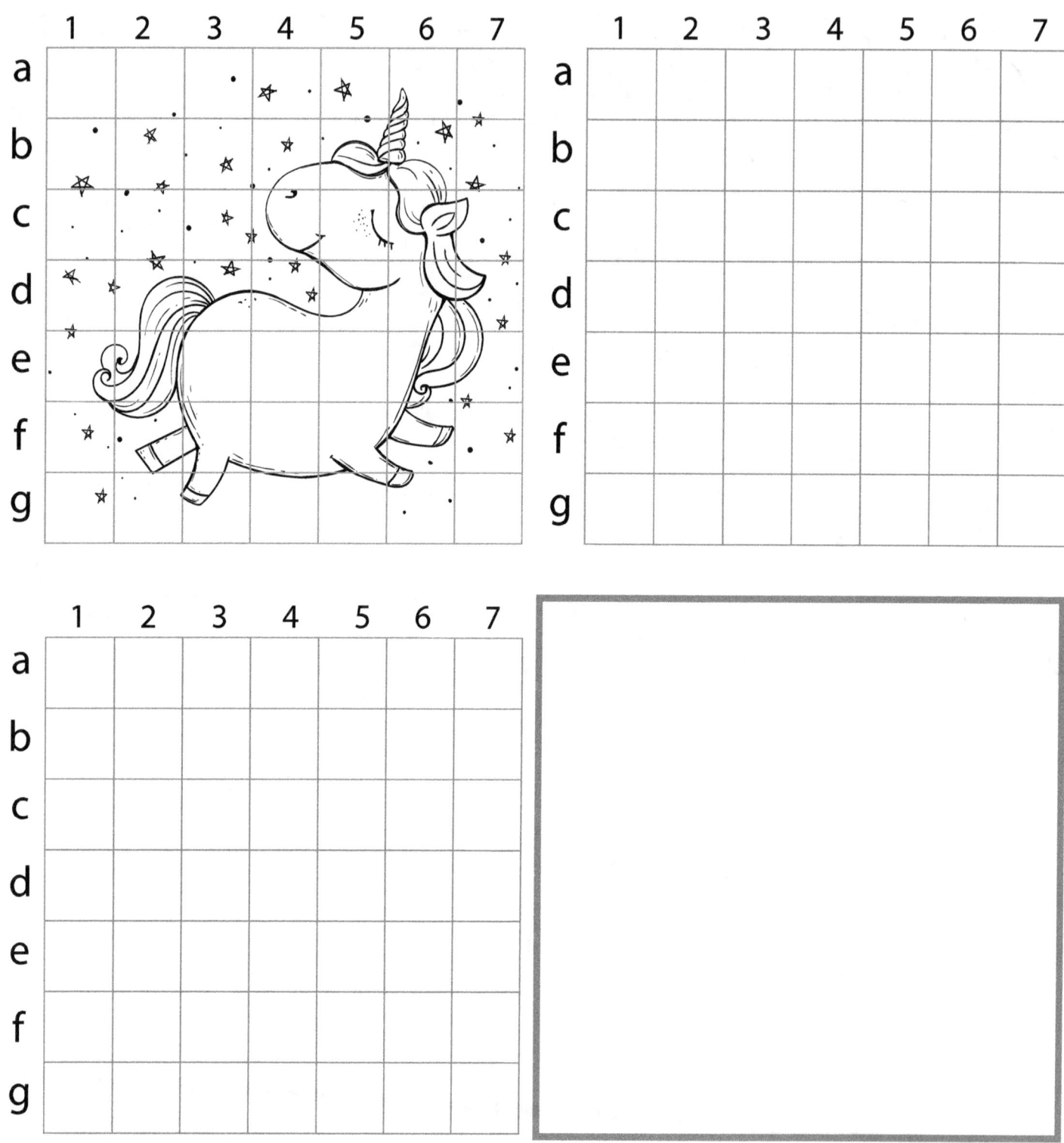

COPY THE BIRD

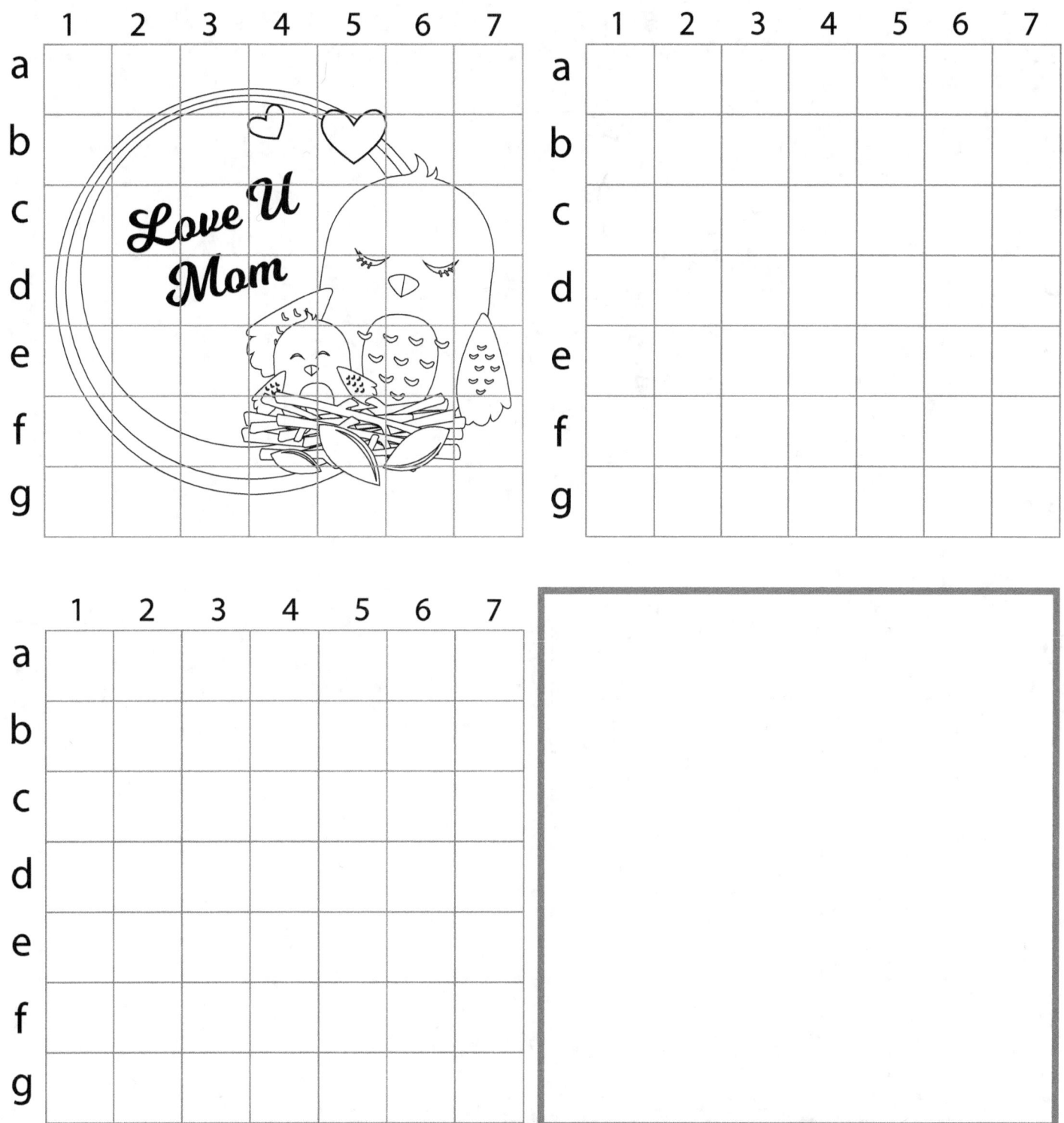

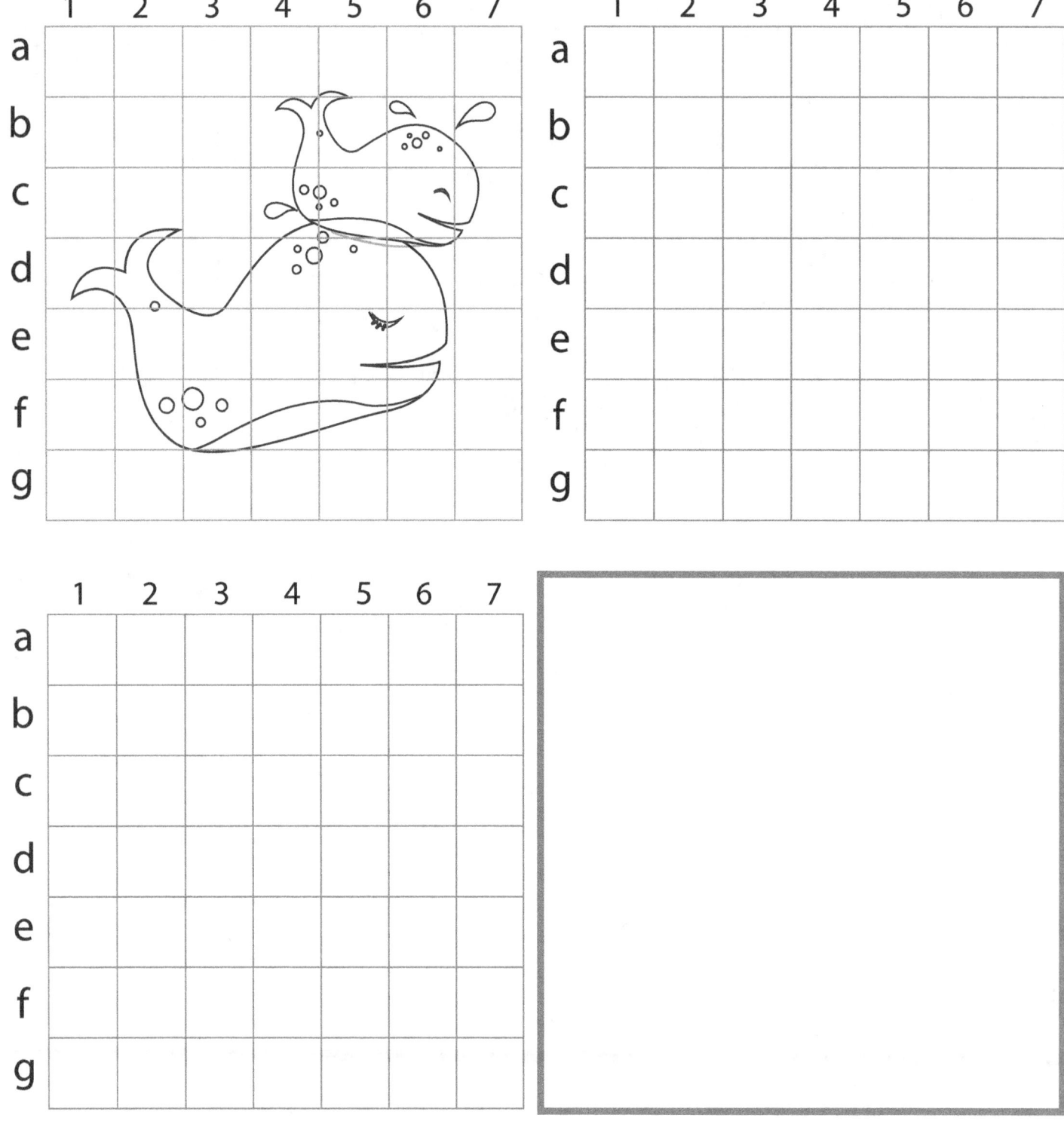

COPY THE ANGLE

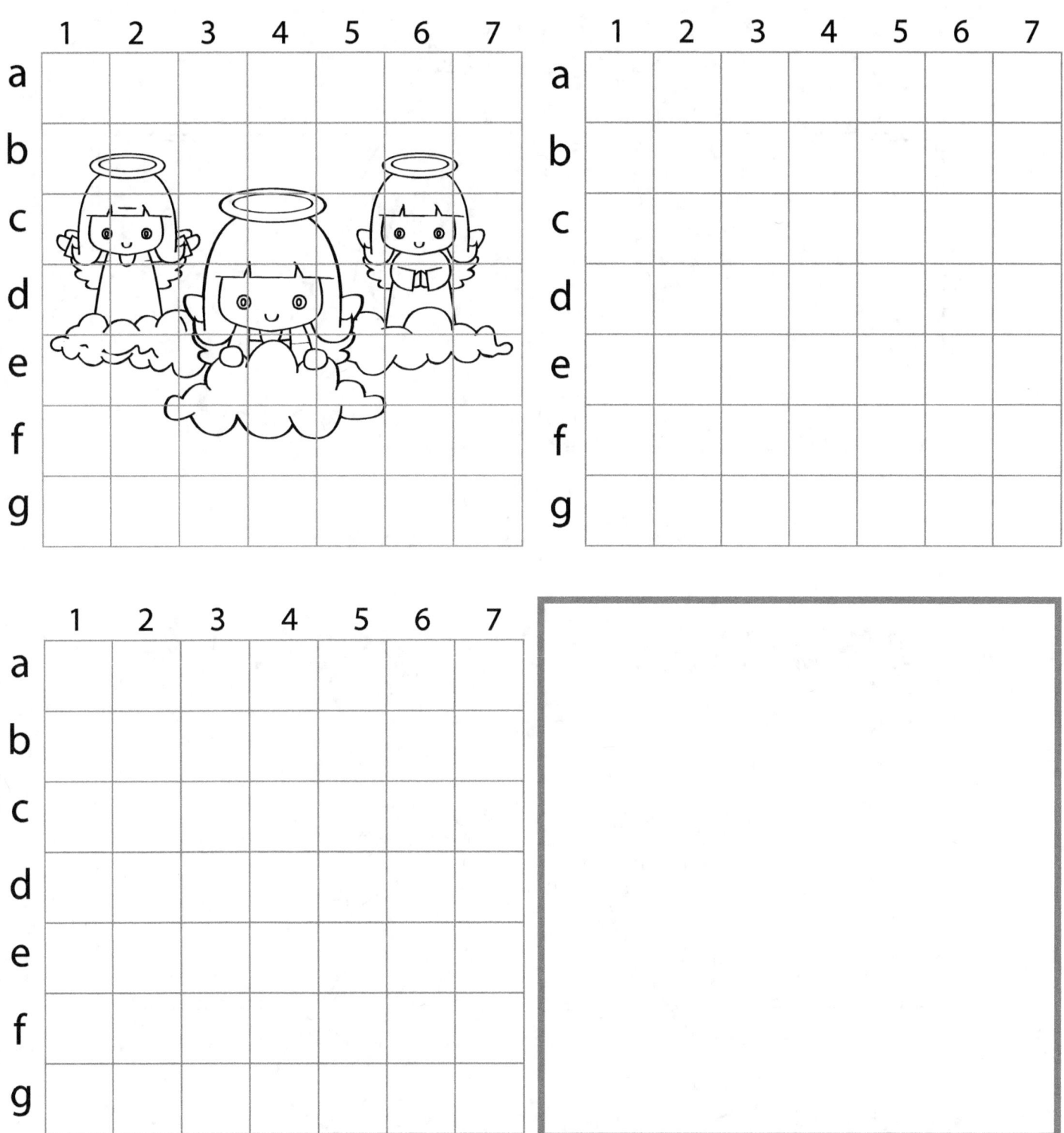

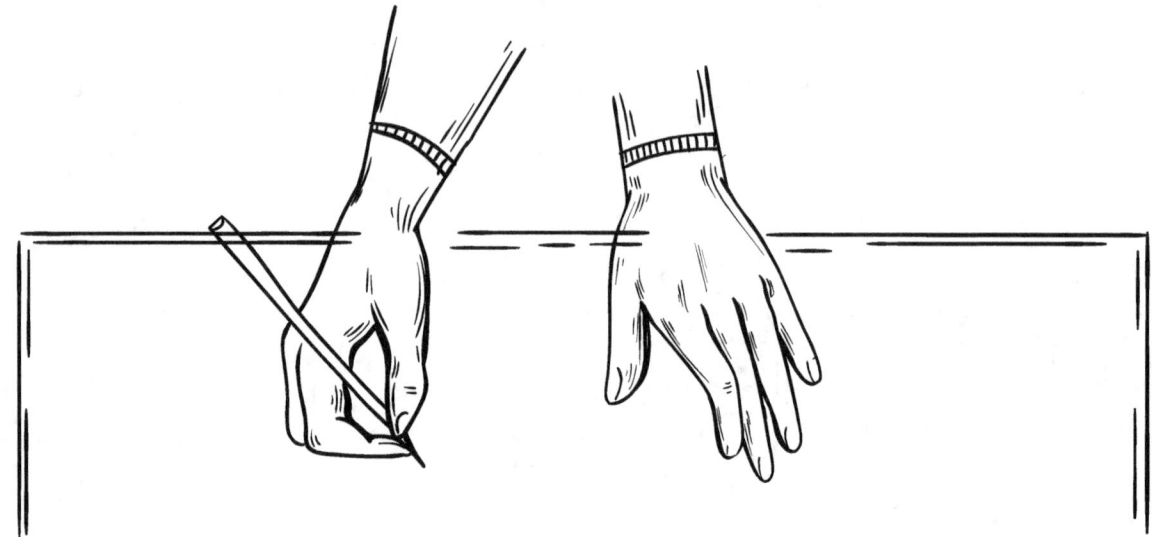

Drawing tutorial step by step repeats the picture.

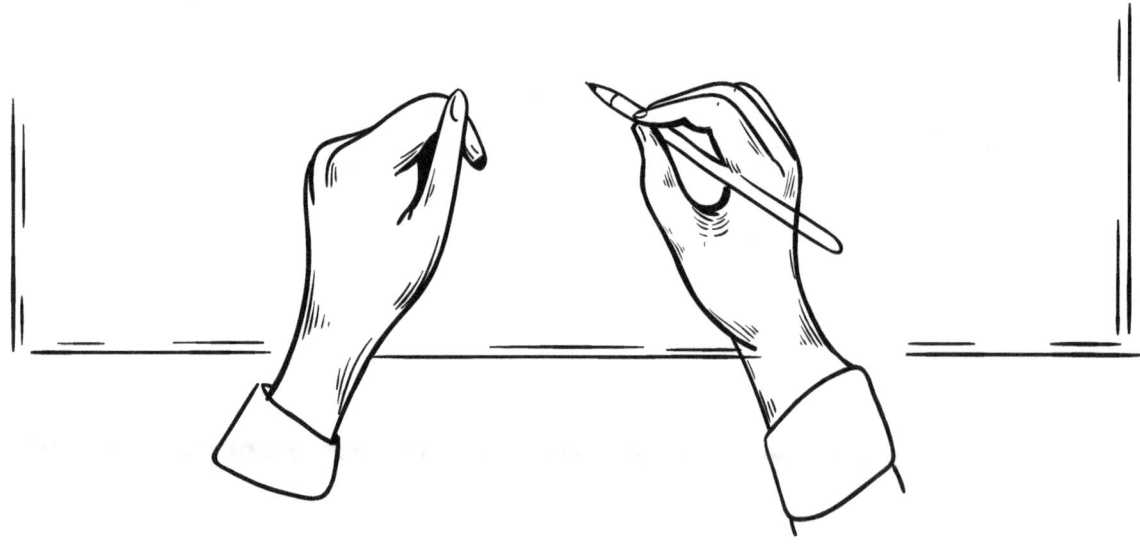

HOW TO DRAW A RABBIT

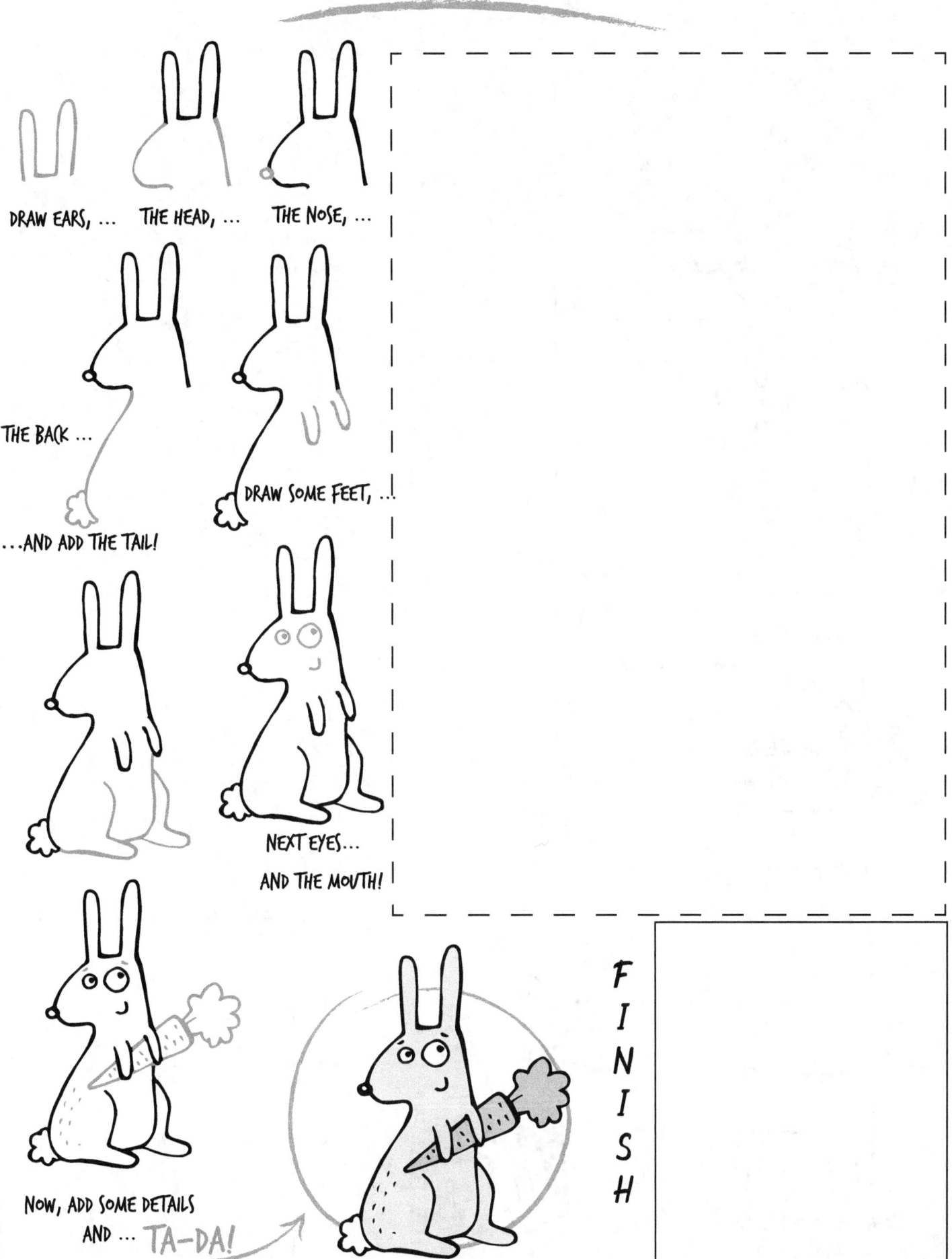

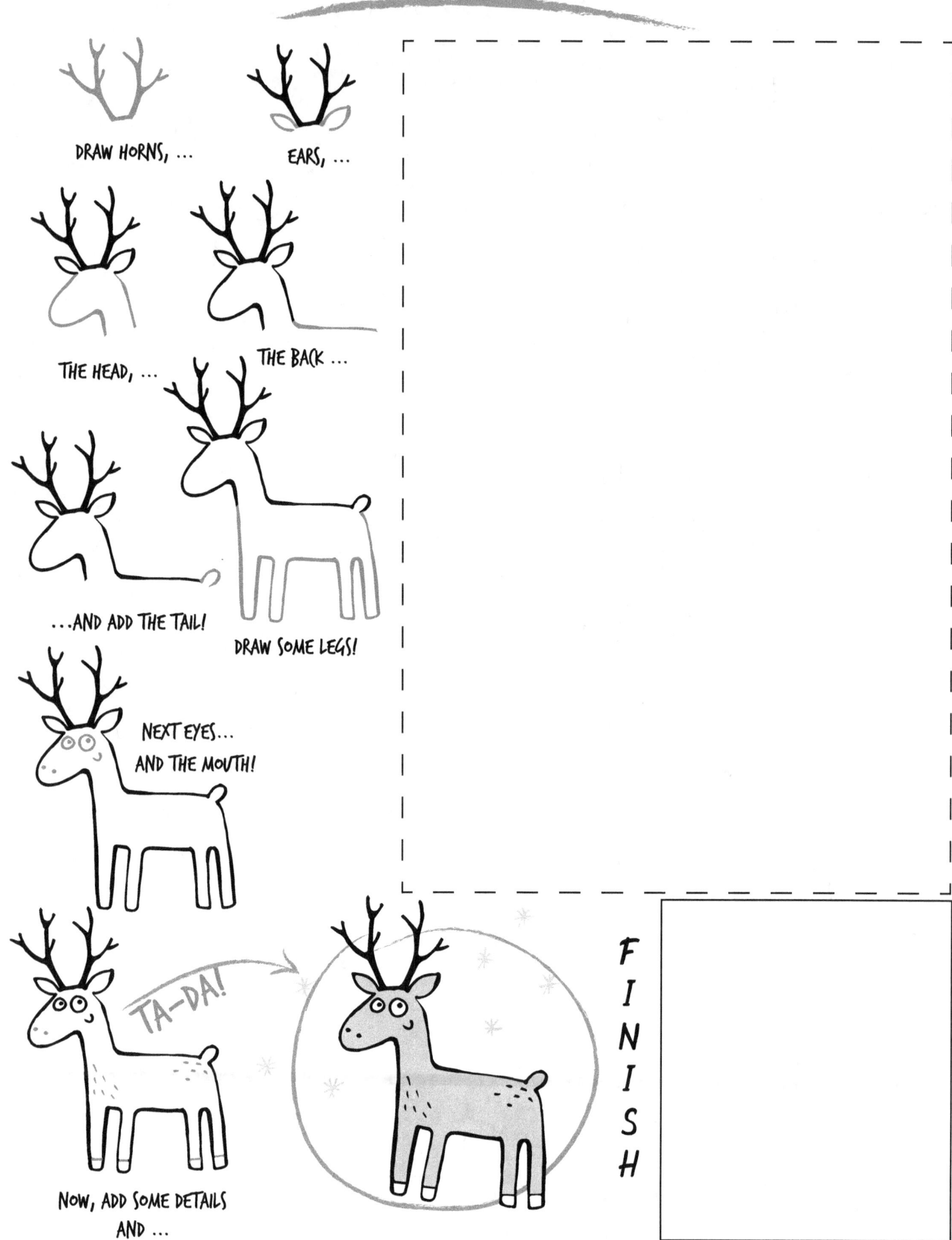

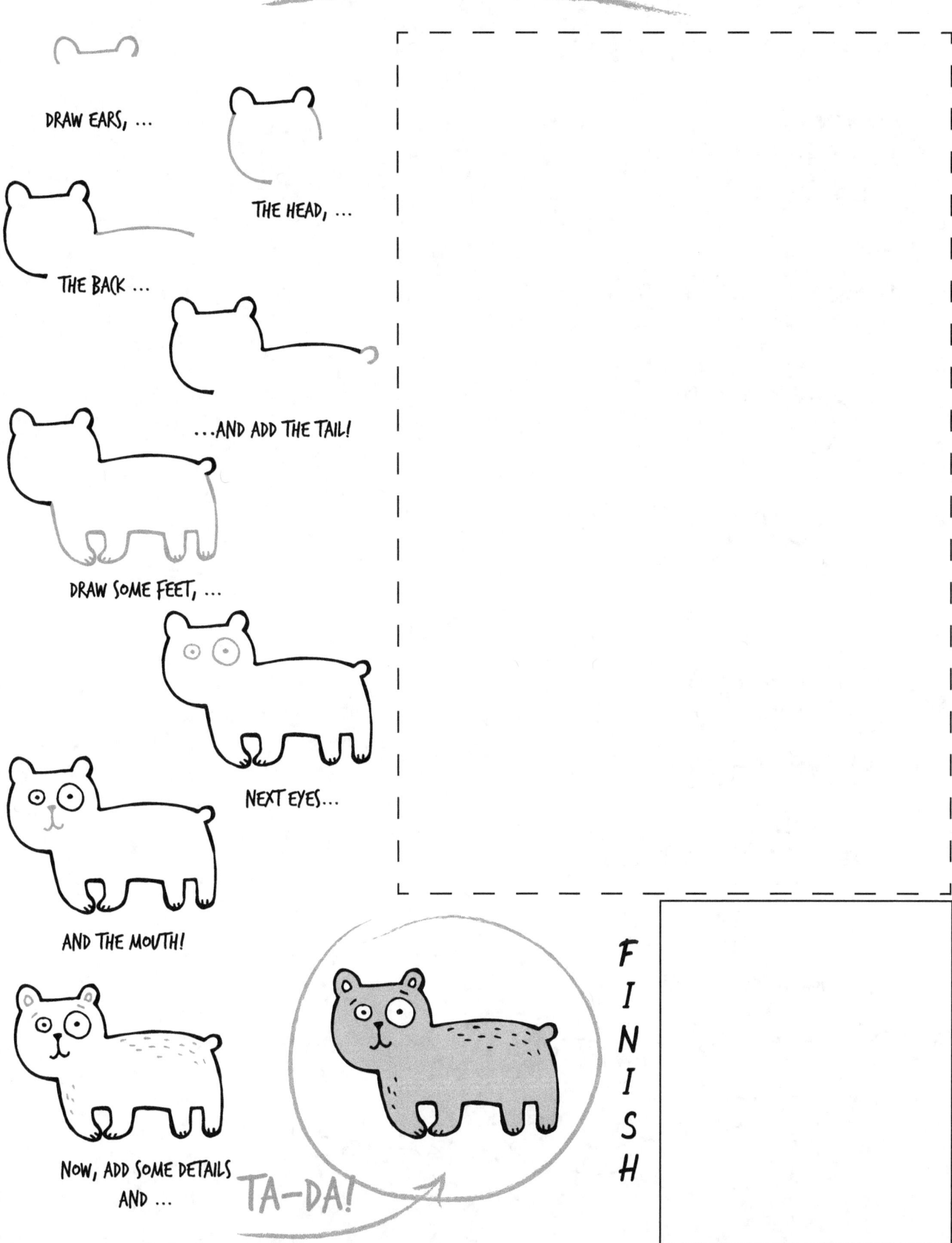

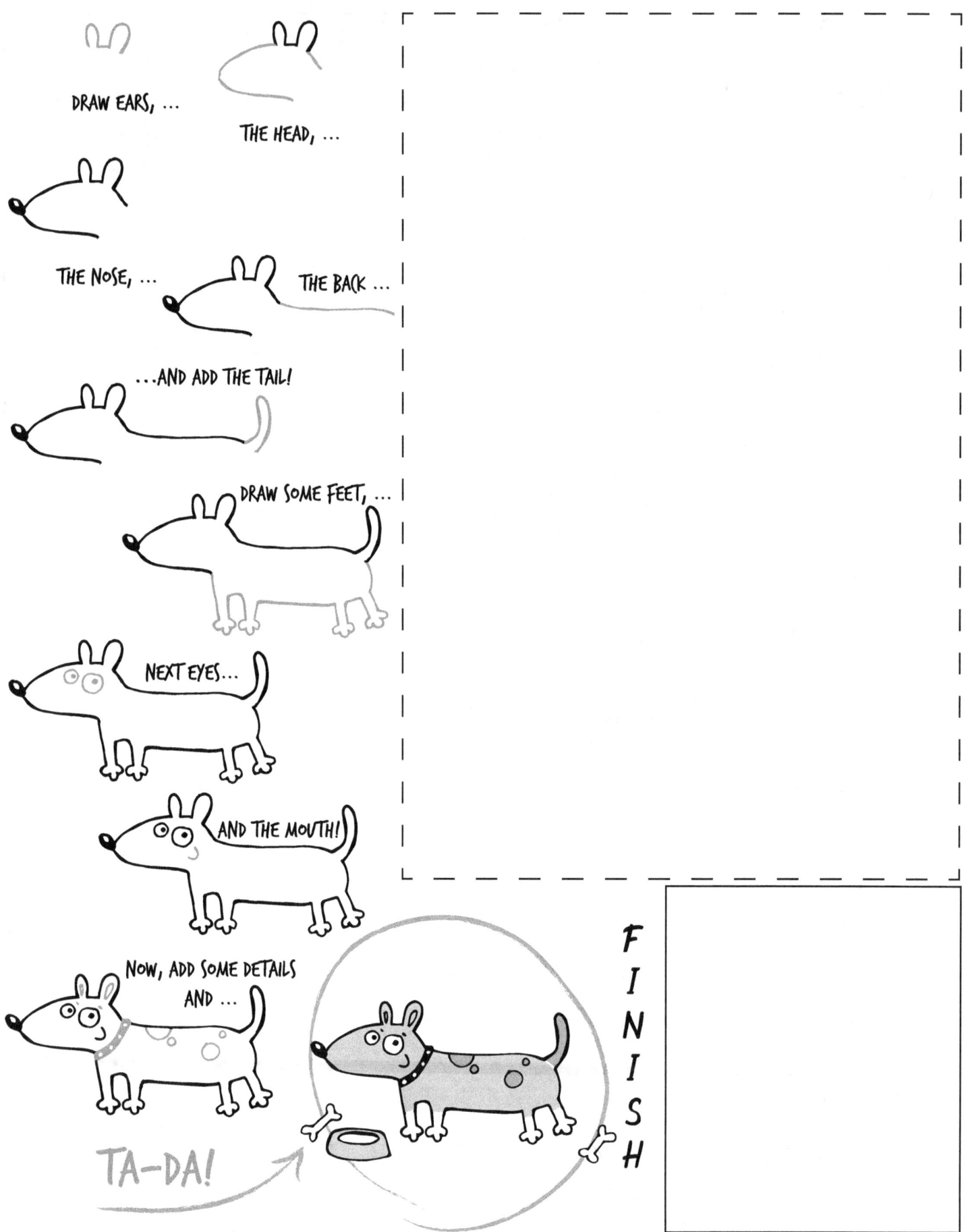

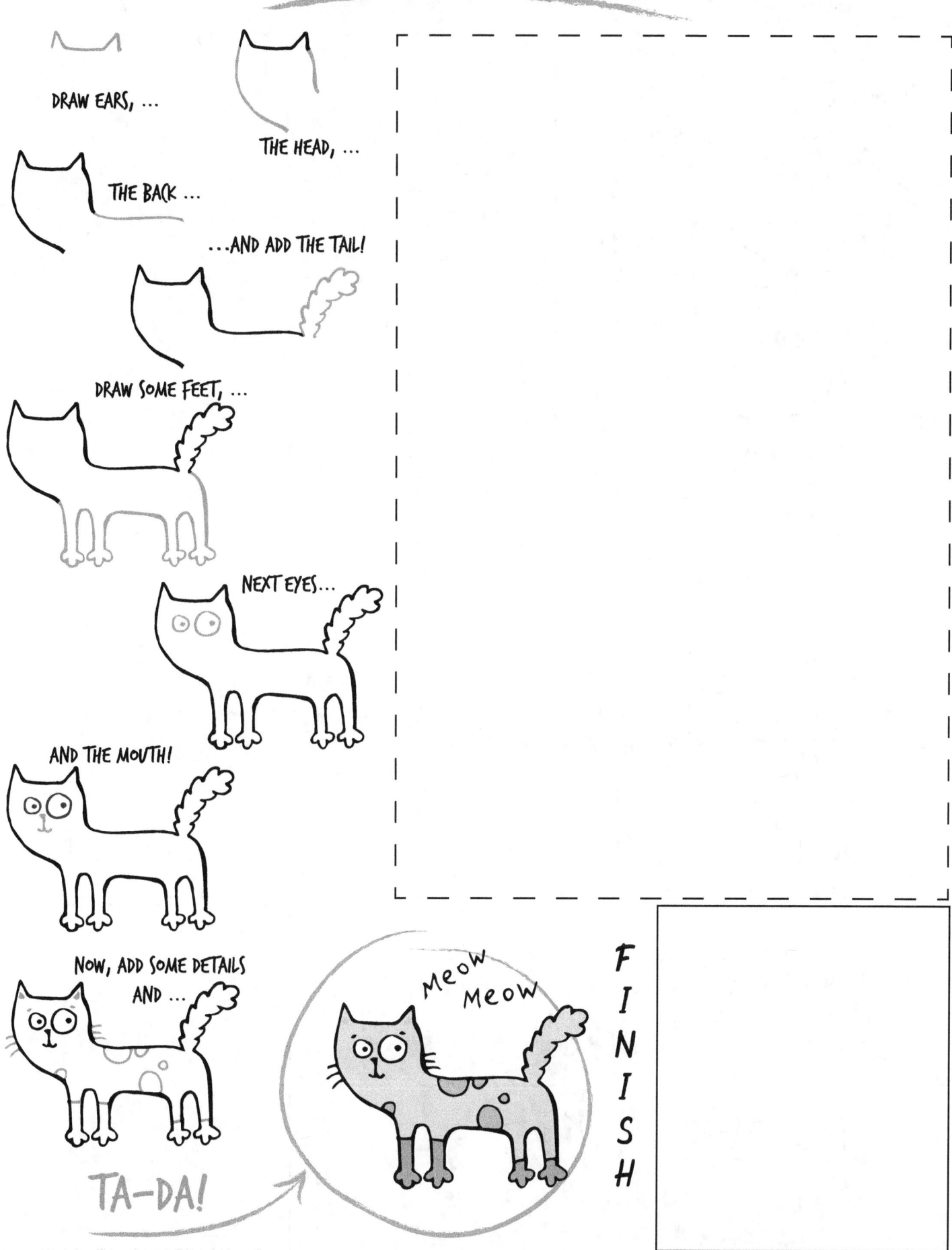

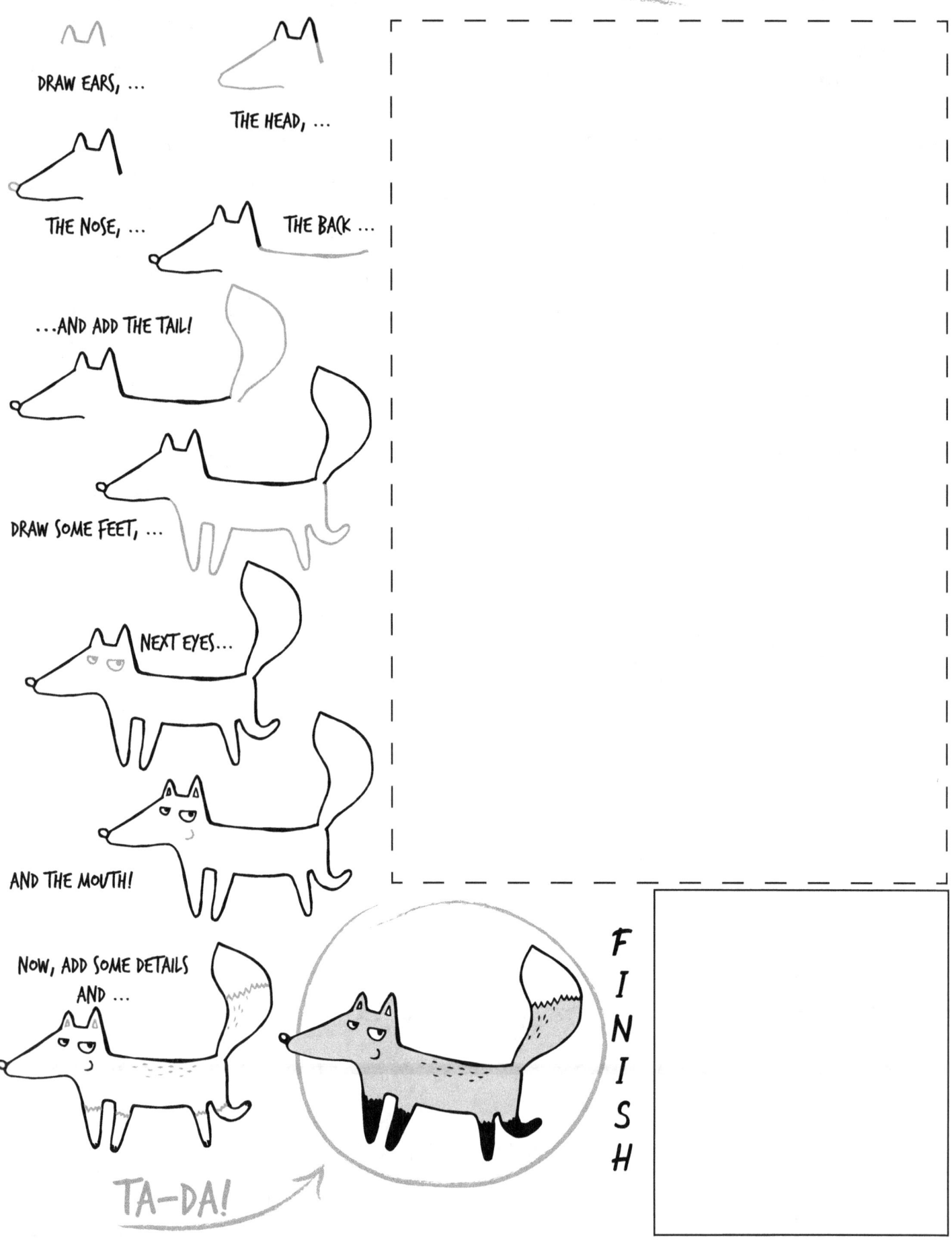

How to draw a CROCODILE

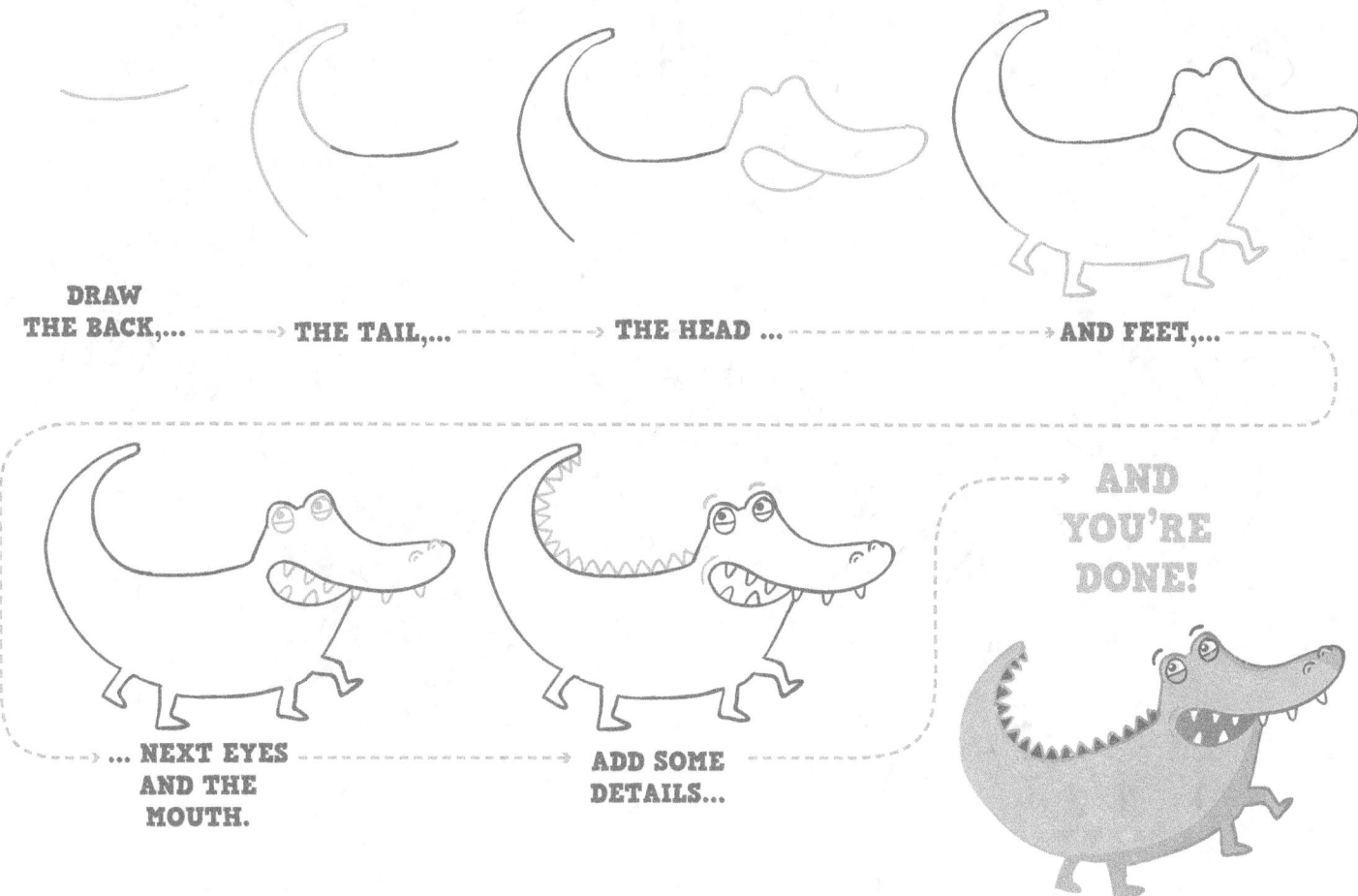

DRAW THE BACK,... → THE TAIL,... → THE HEAD ... → AND FEET,... → ... NEXT EYES AND THE MOUTH. → ADD SOME DETAILS... → AND YOU'RE DONE!

How to draw a ROSE

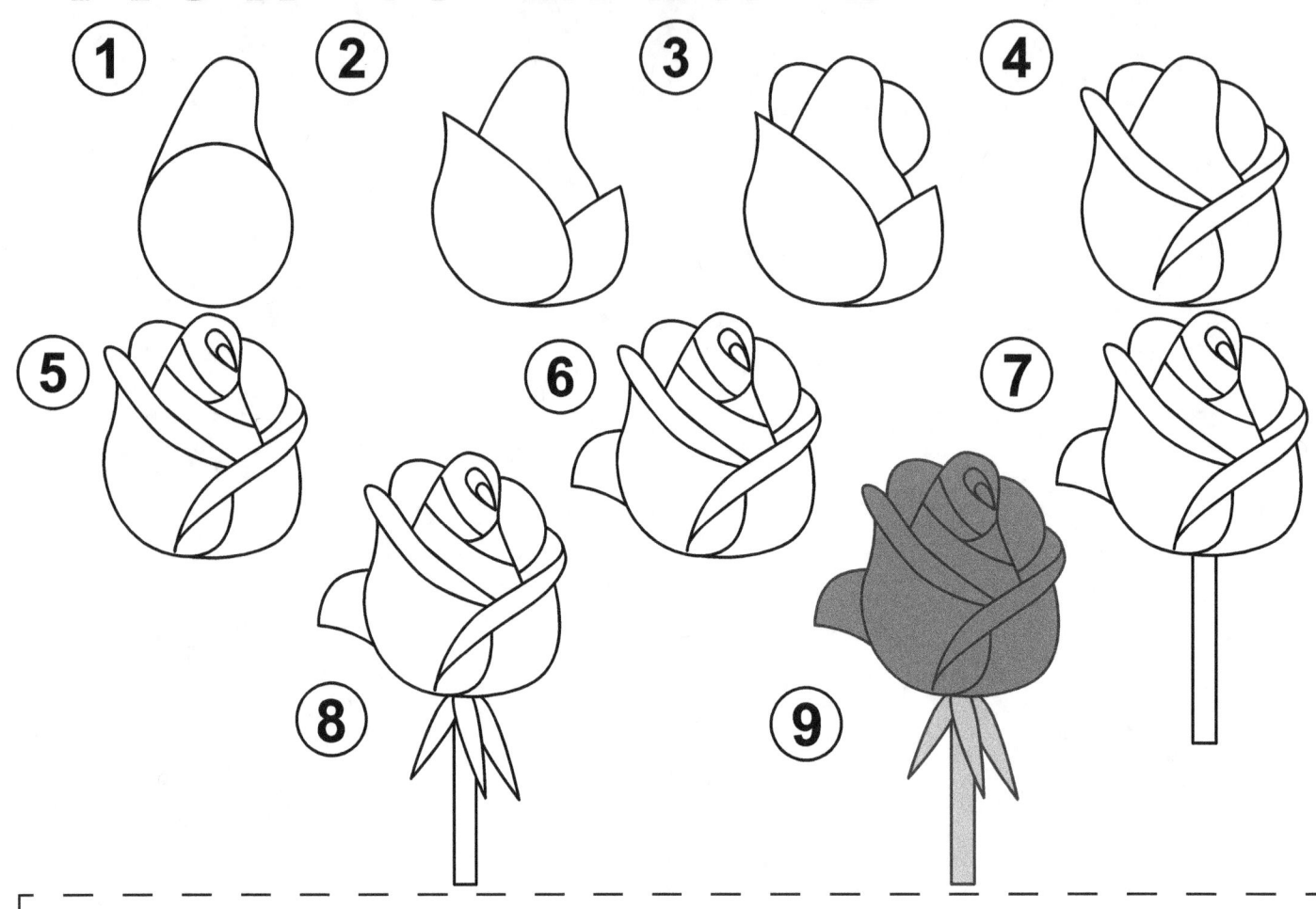

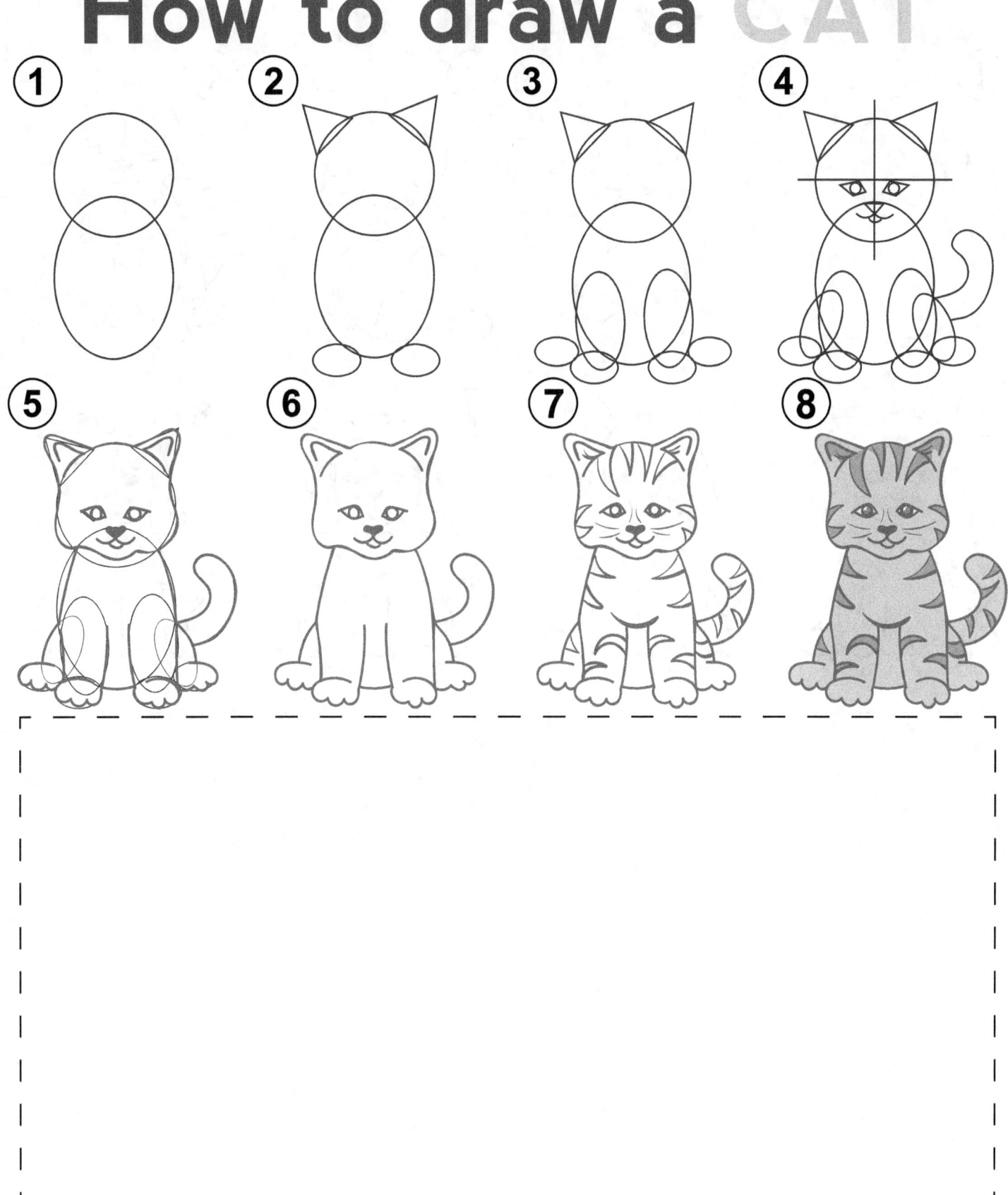

How to draw a DOG

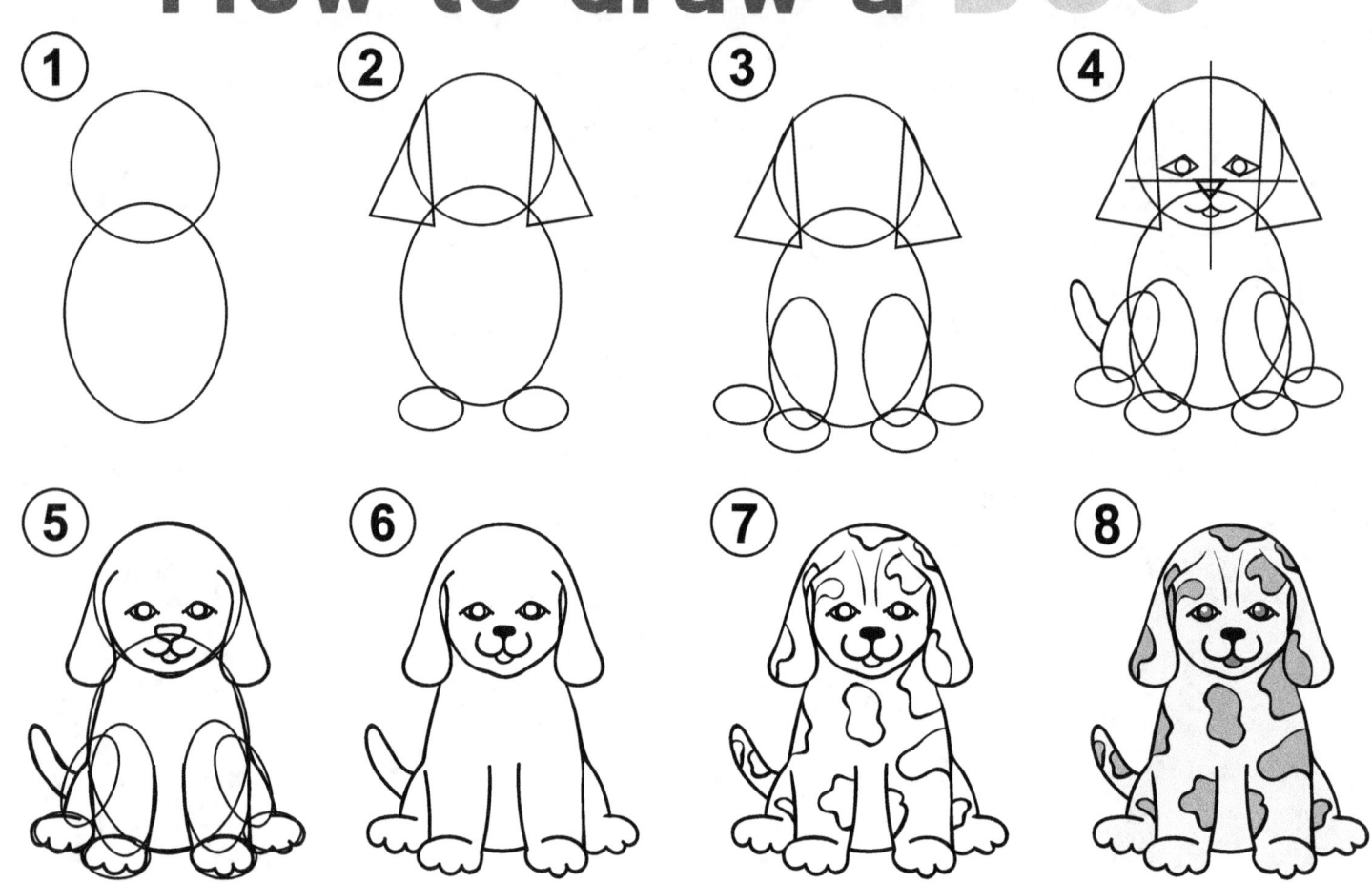

How to draw a RIBBIN BOW

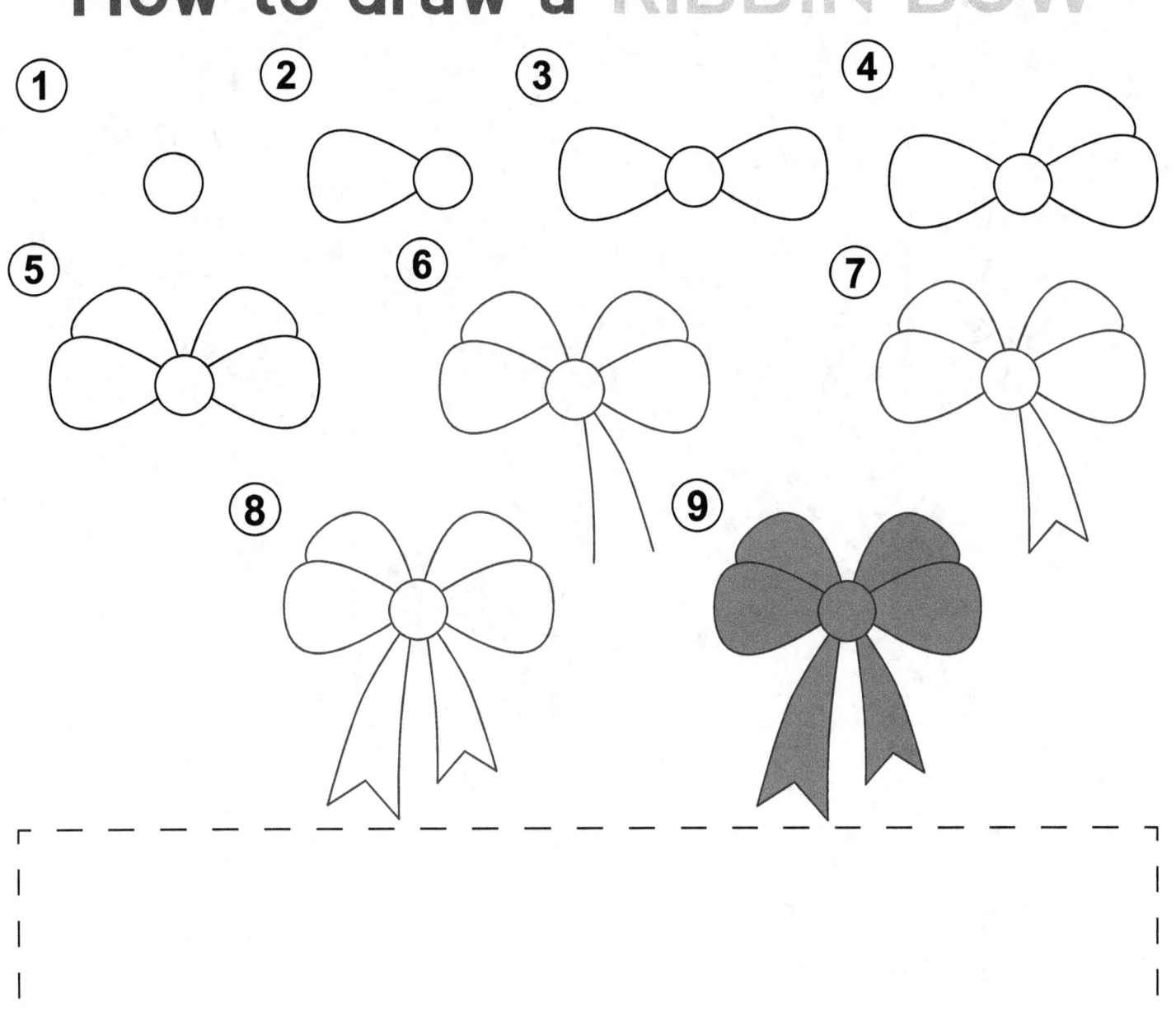

How to draw a PENGUIN

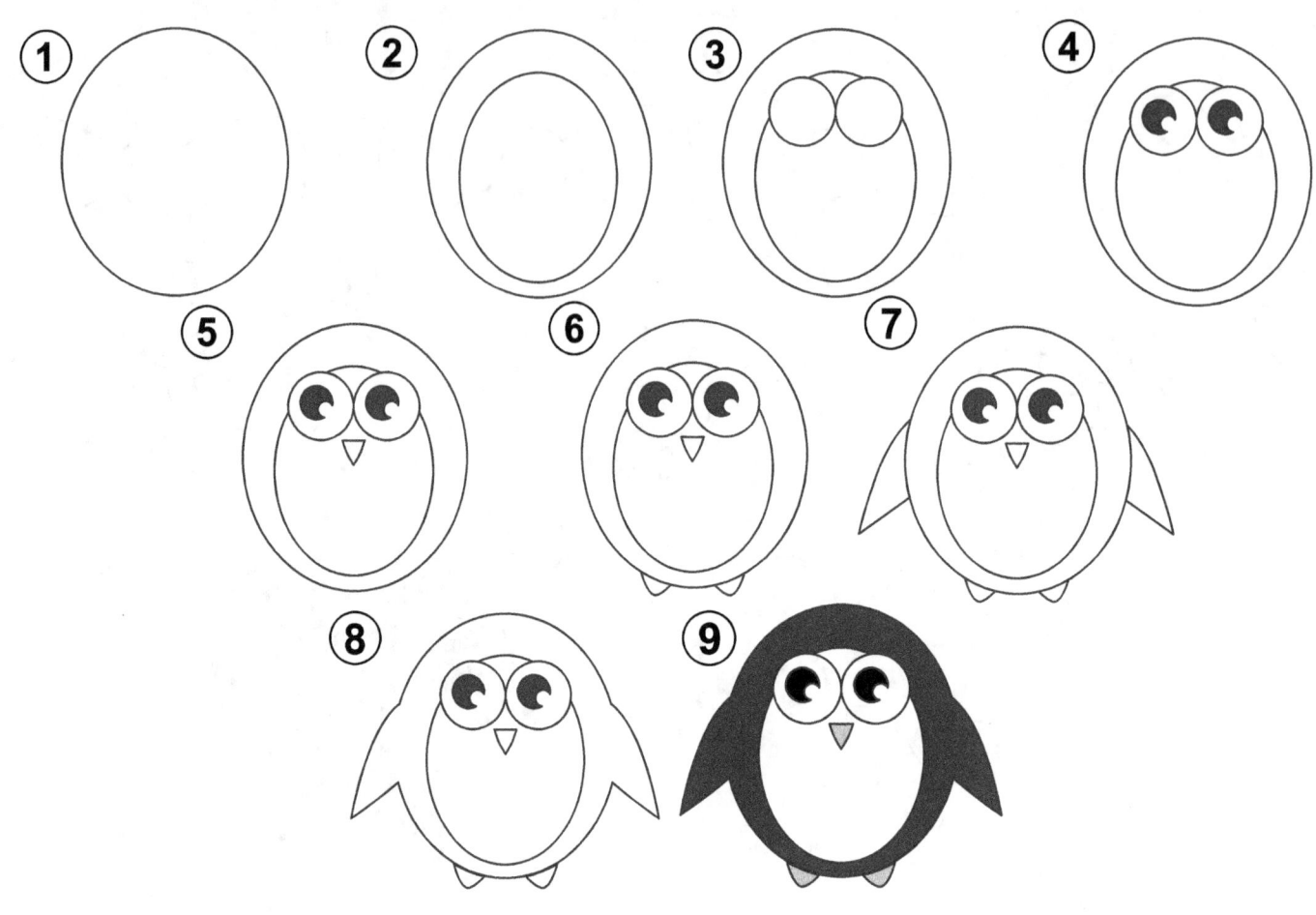

How to draw a CAT

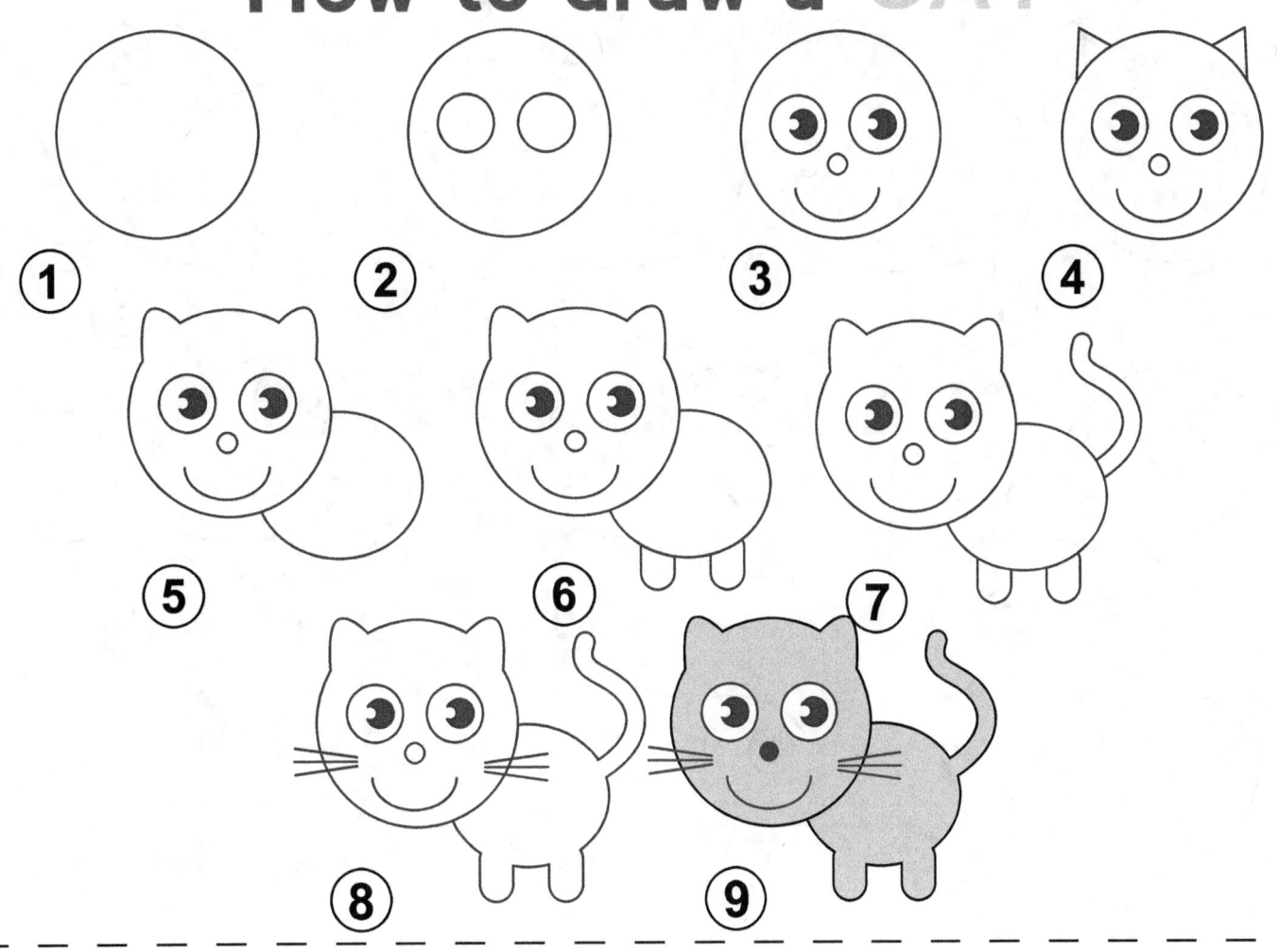

How to draw a FISH

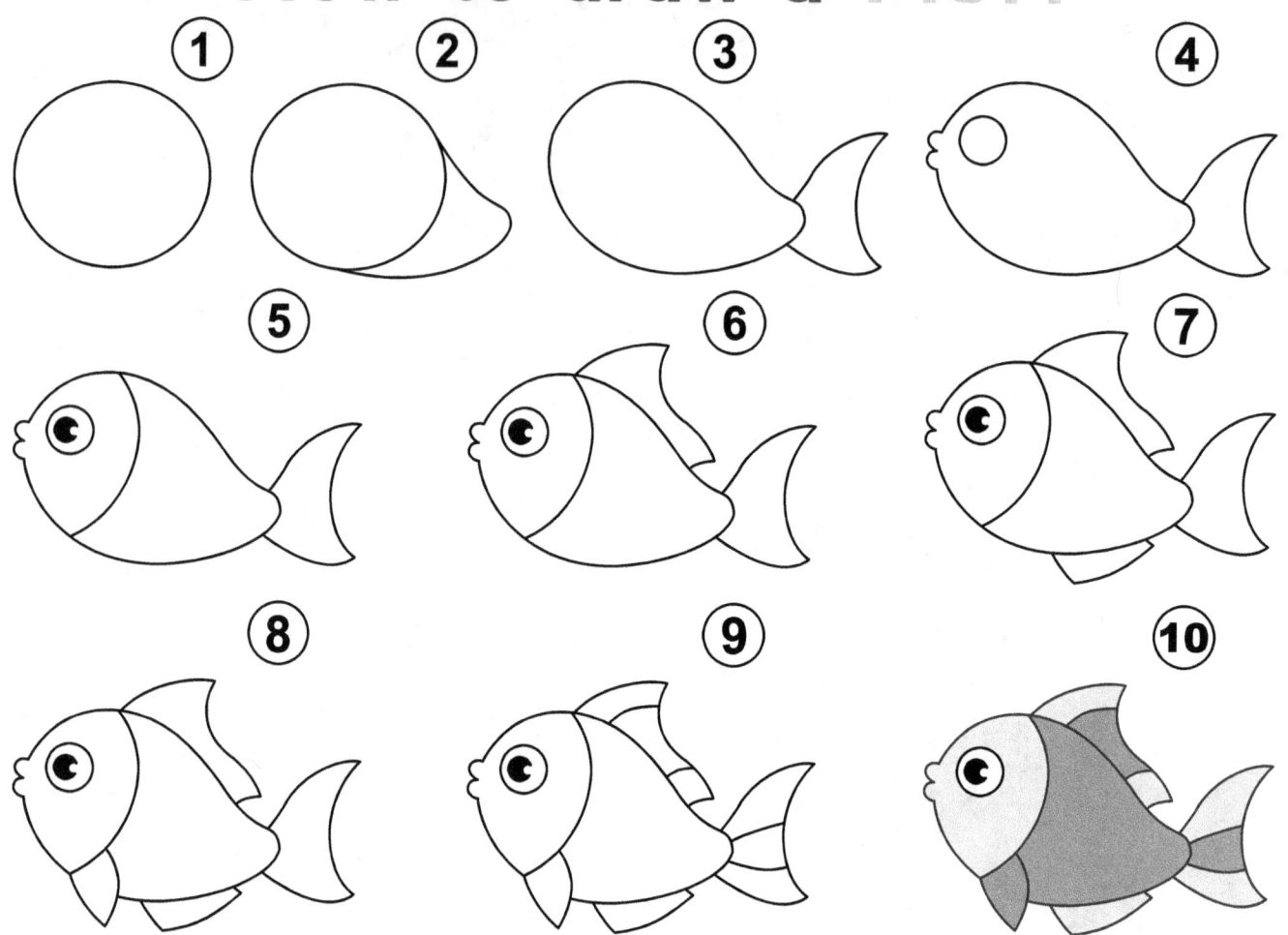

How to draw a CRAB

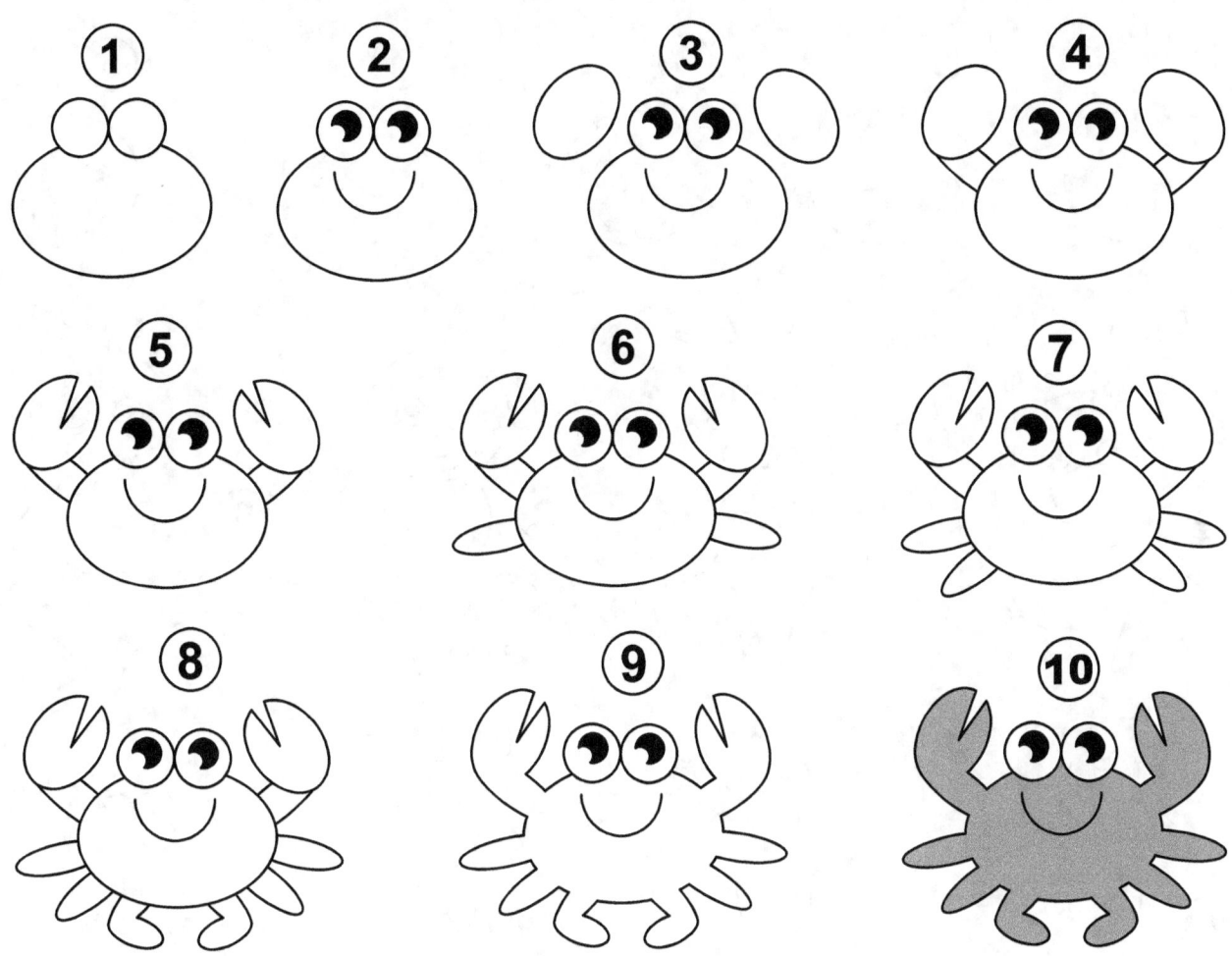

How to draw a RABBIT

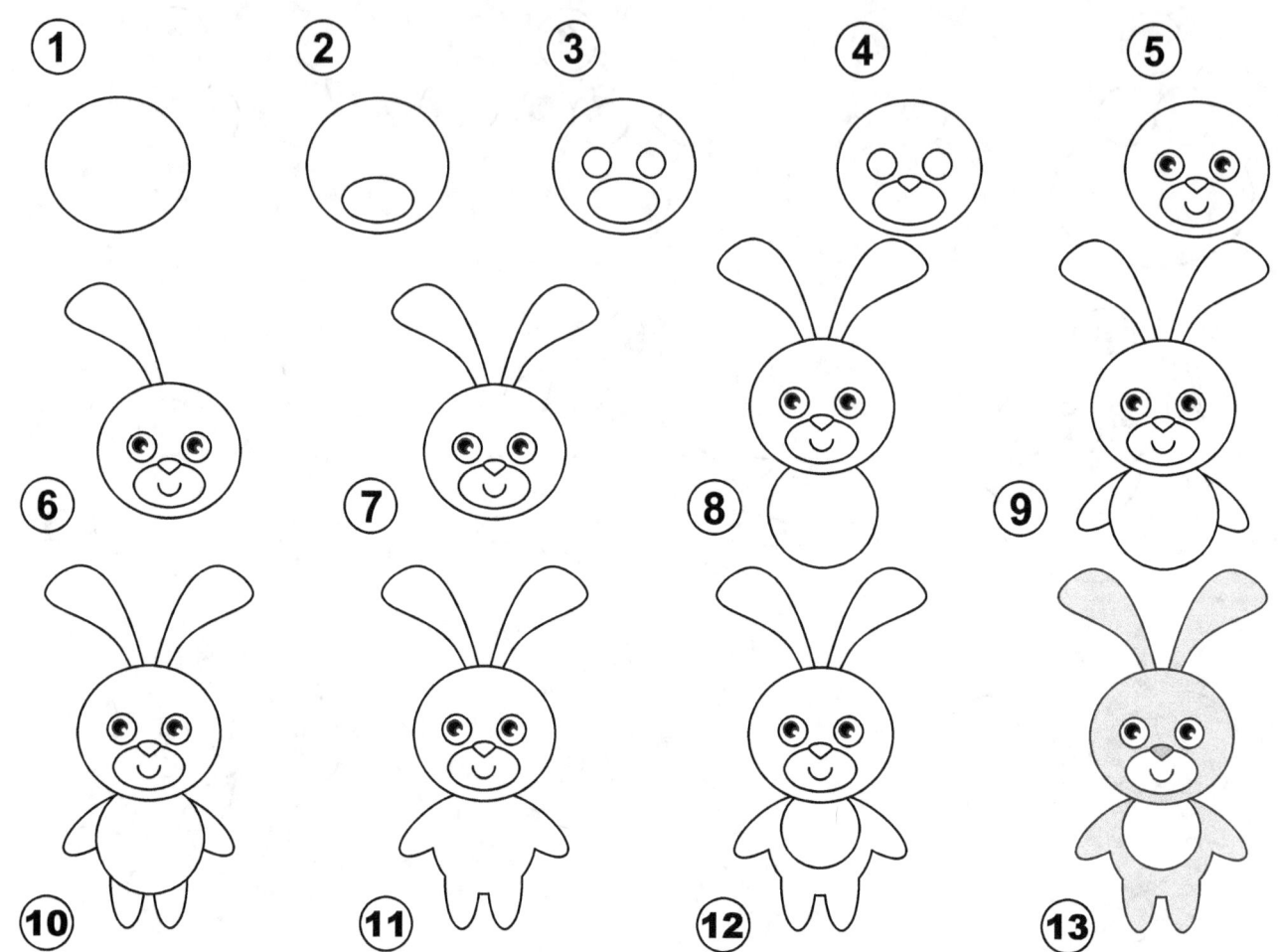

How to draw a ZEBRA

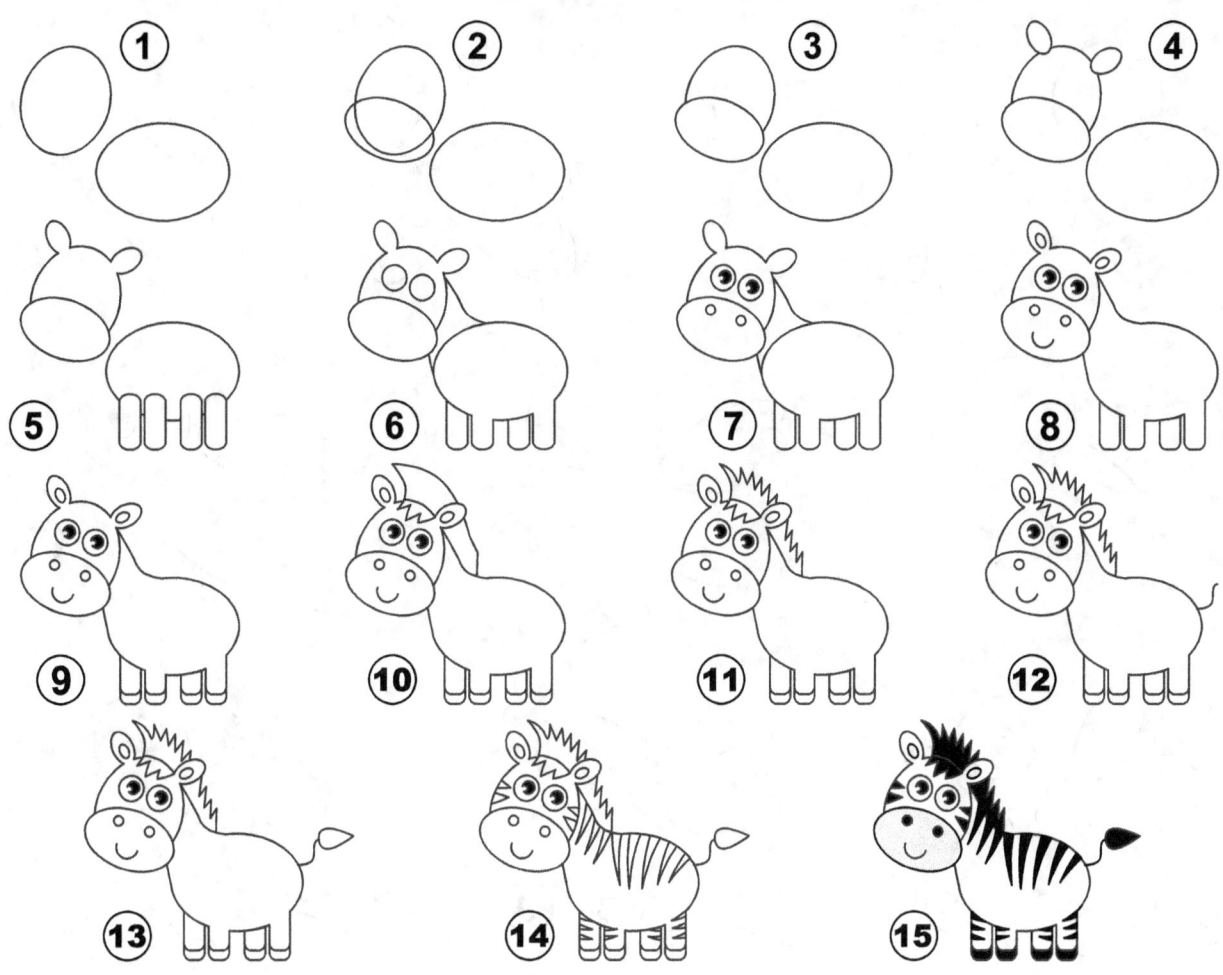

How to draw a ZEBRA

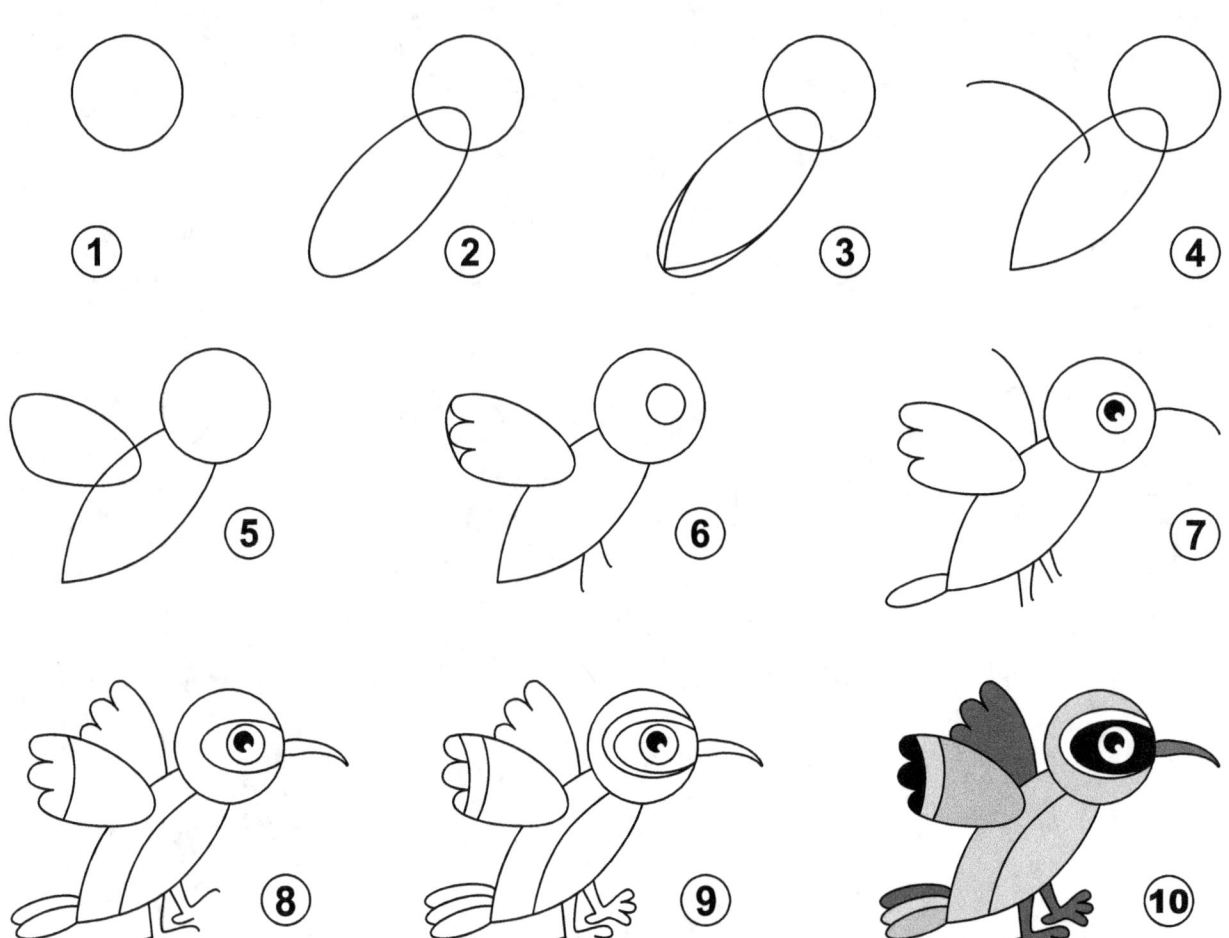

How to draw a SQUIRREL

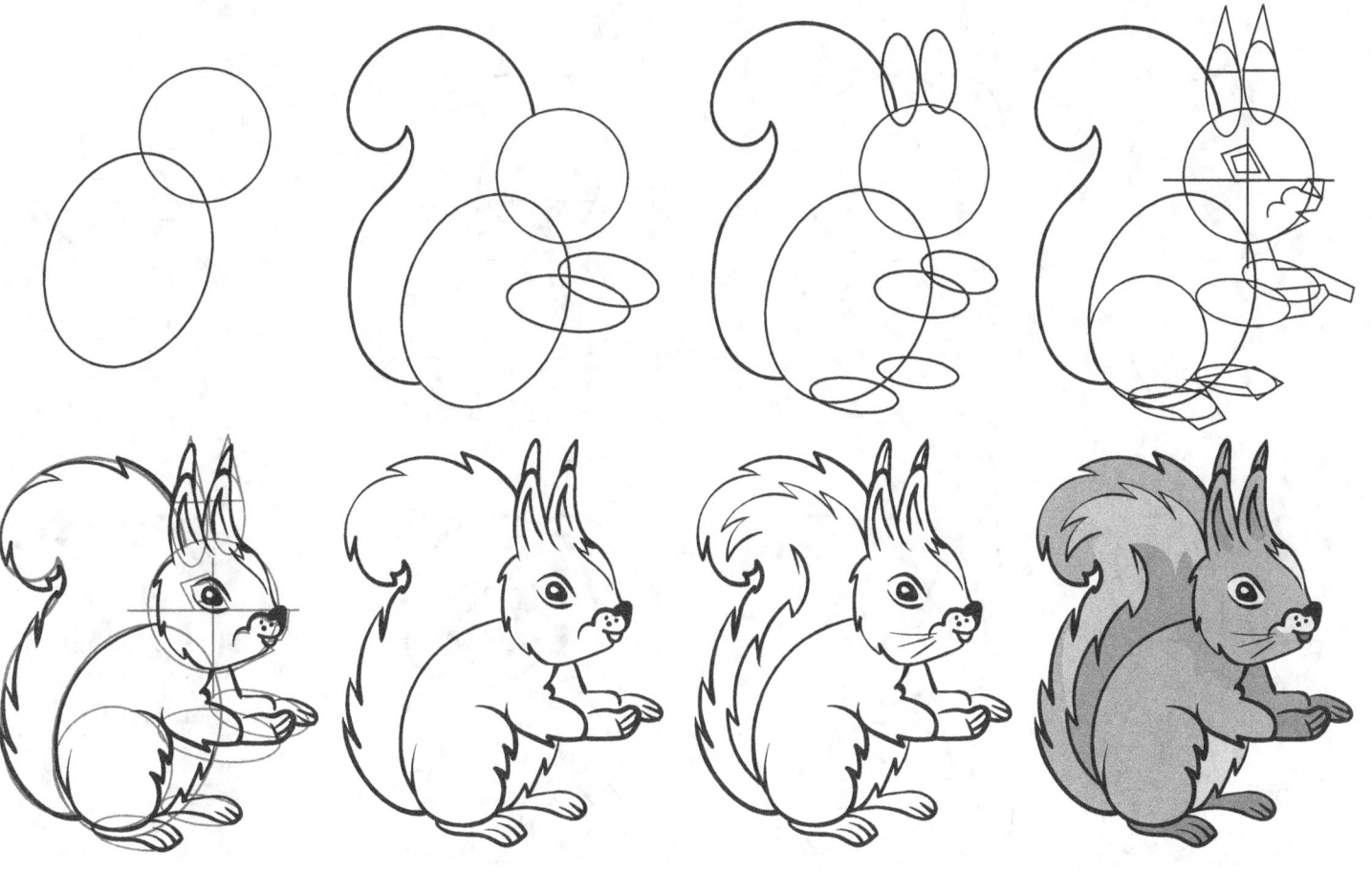

How to draw a PANDA

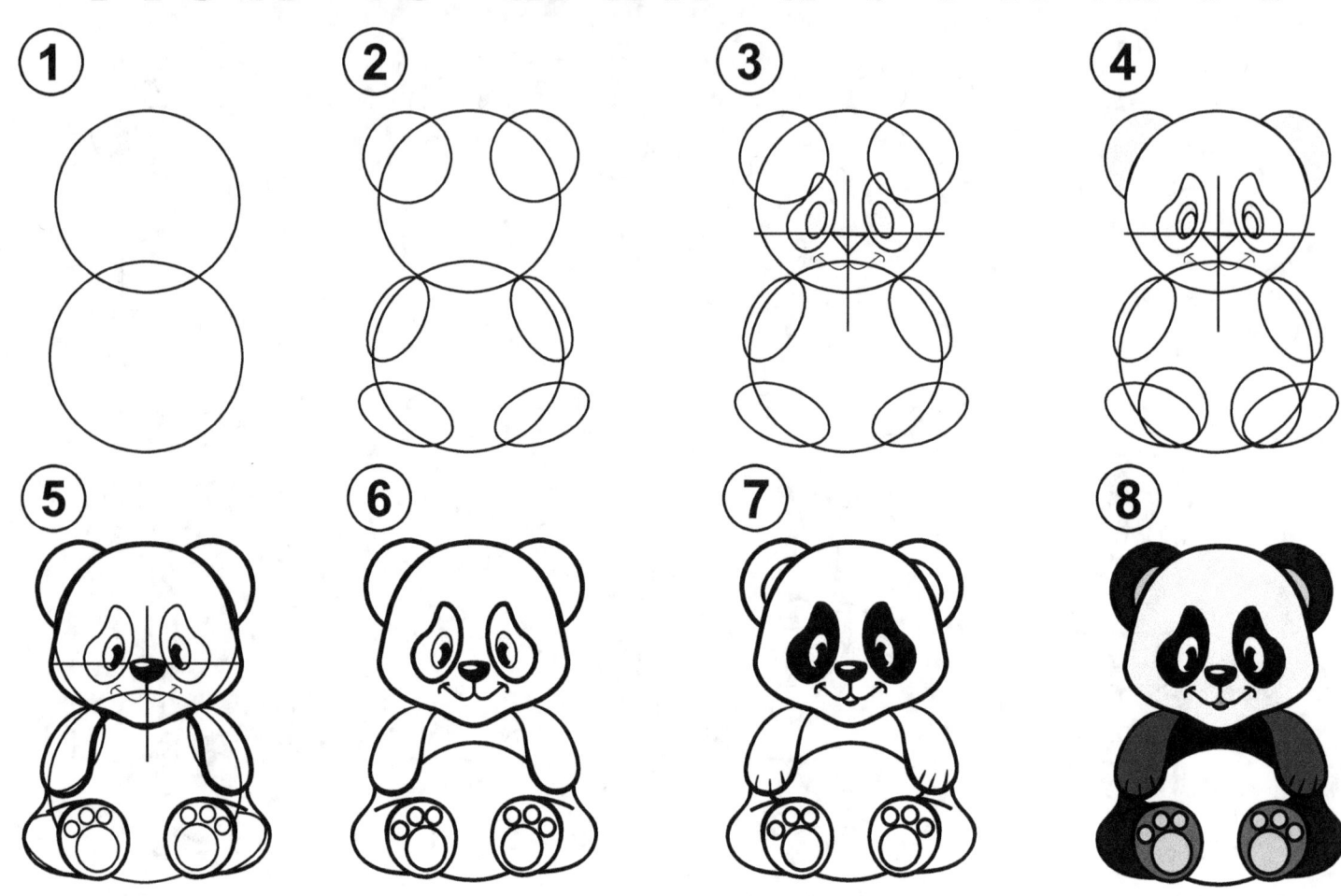

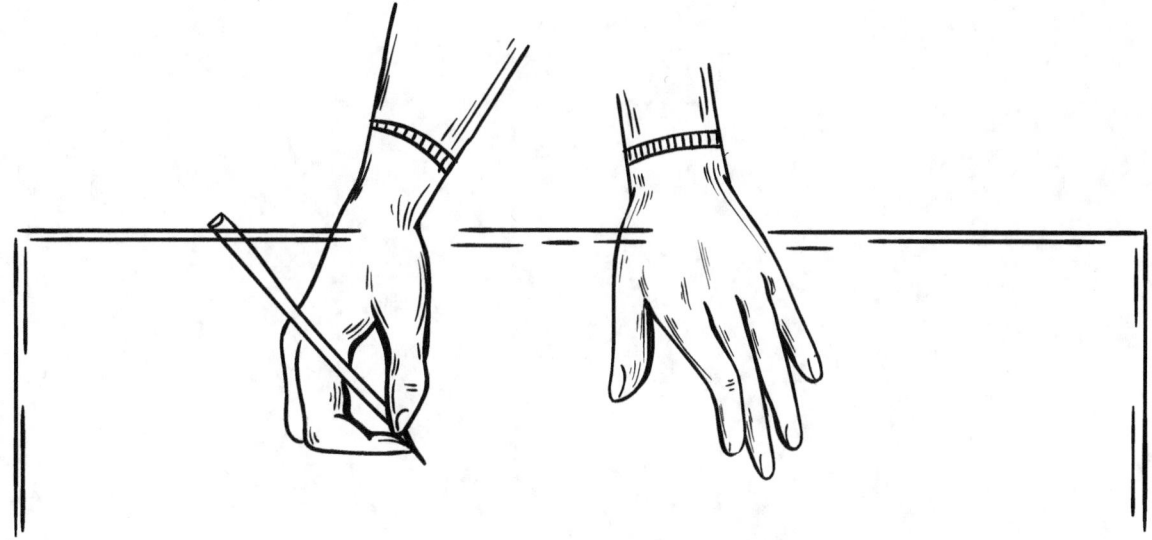

DRAWING PAD & FRAME

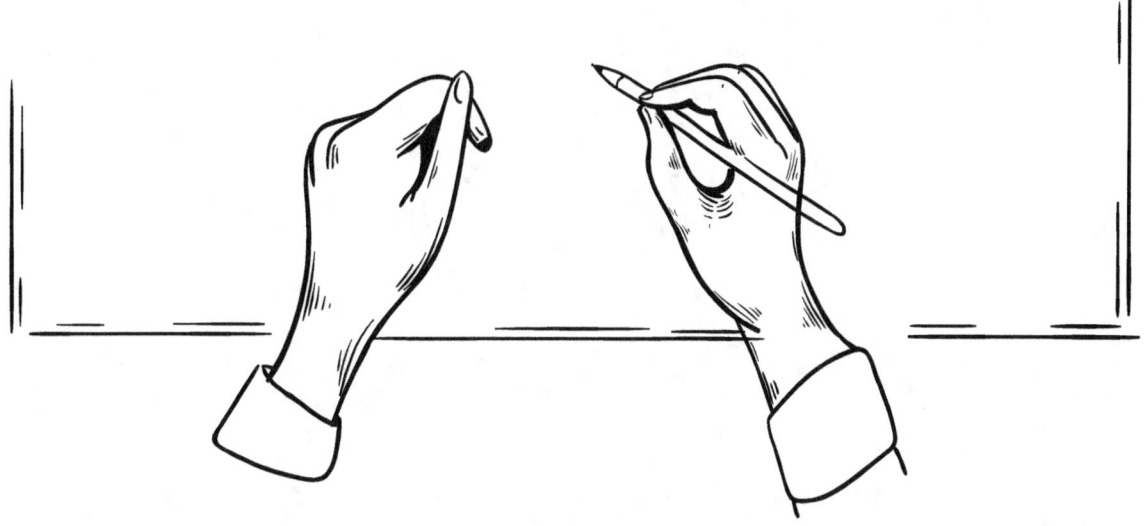

DRAWING PAD

DRAWING PAD

DRAWING PAD

DRAWING PAD

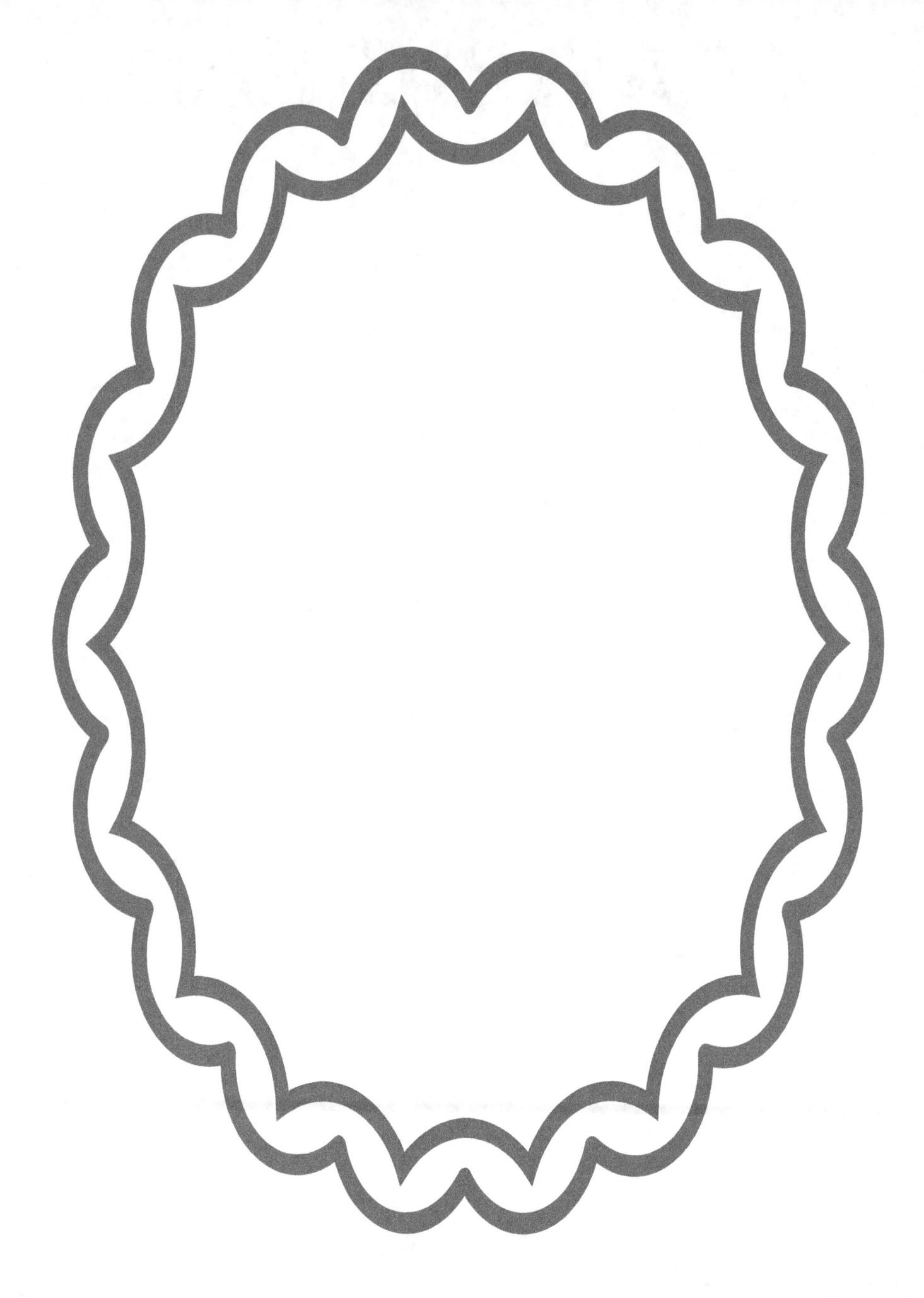

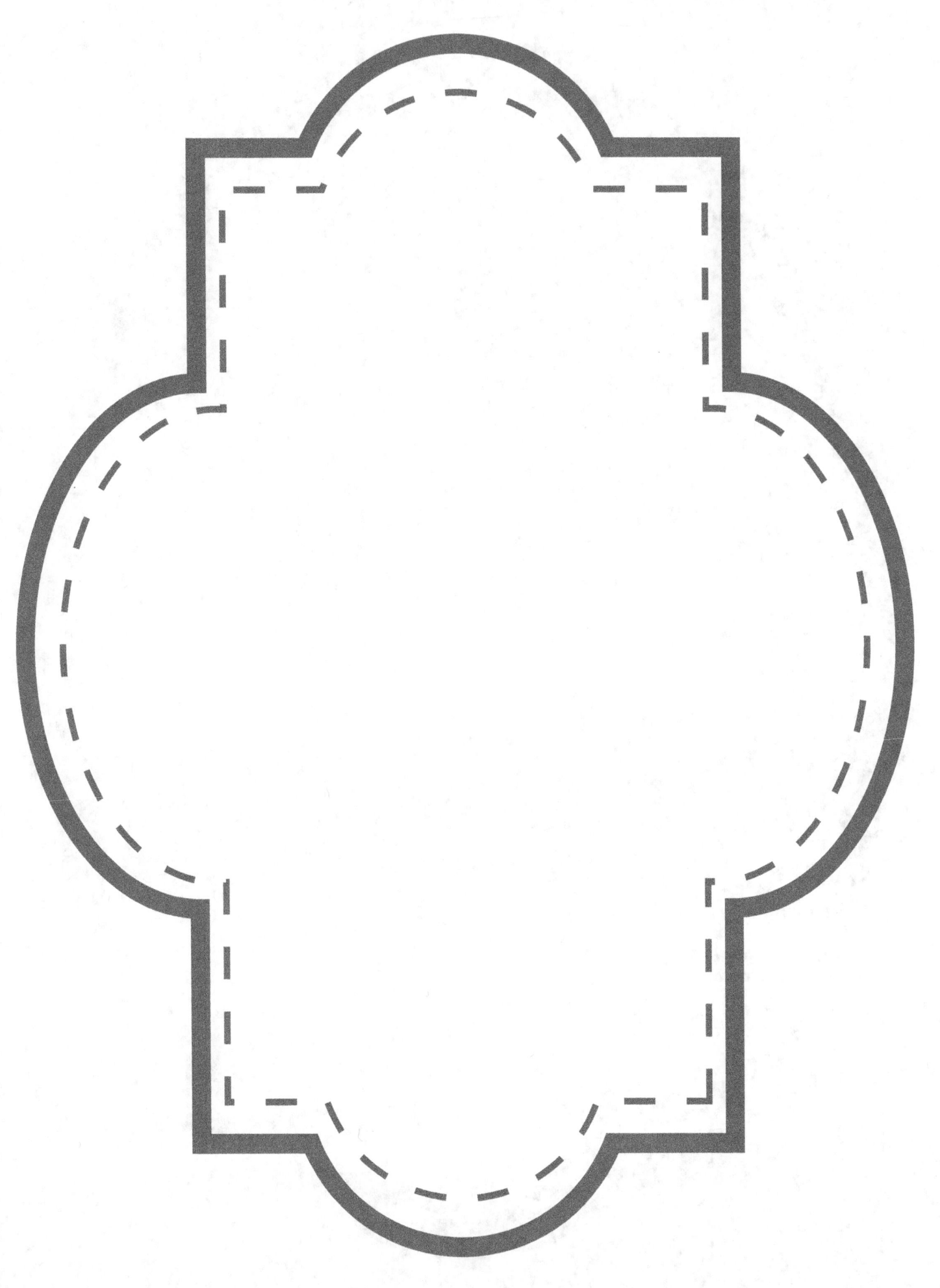

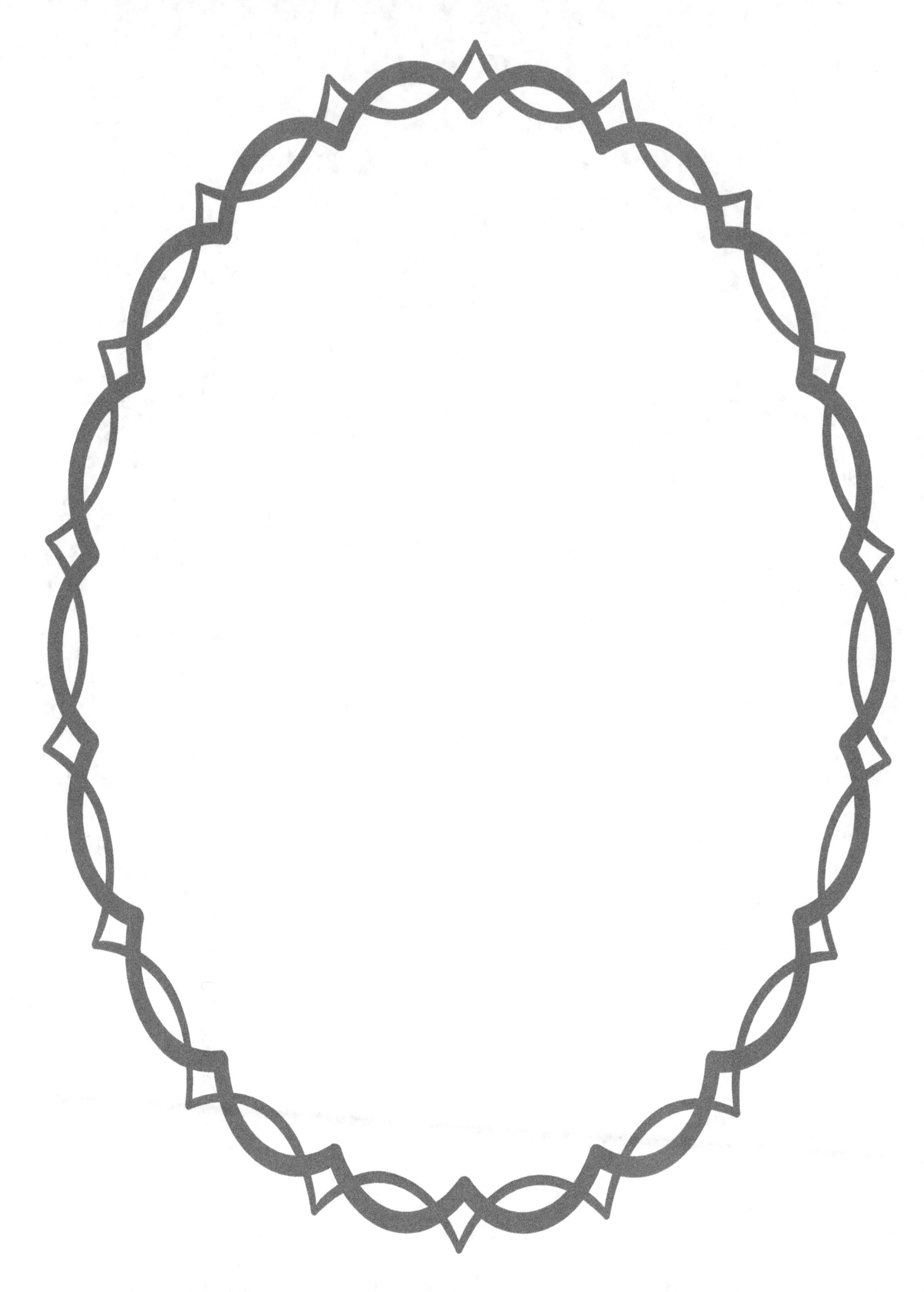

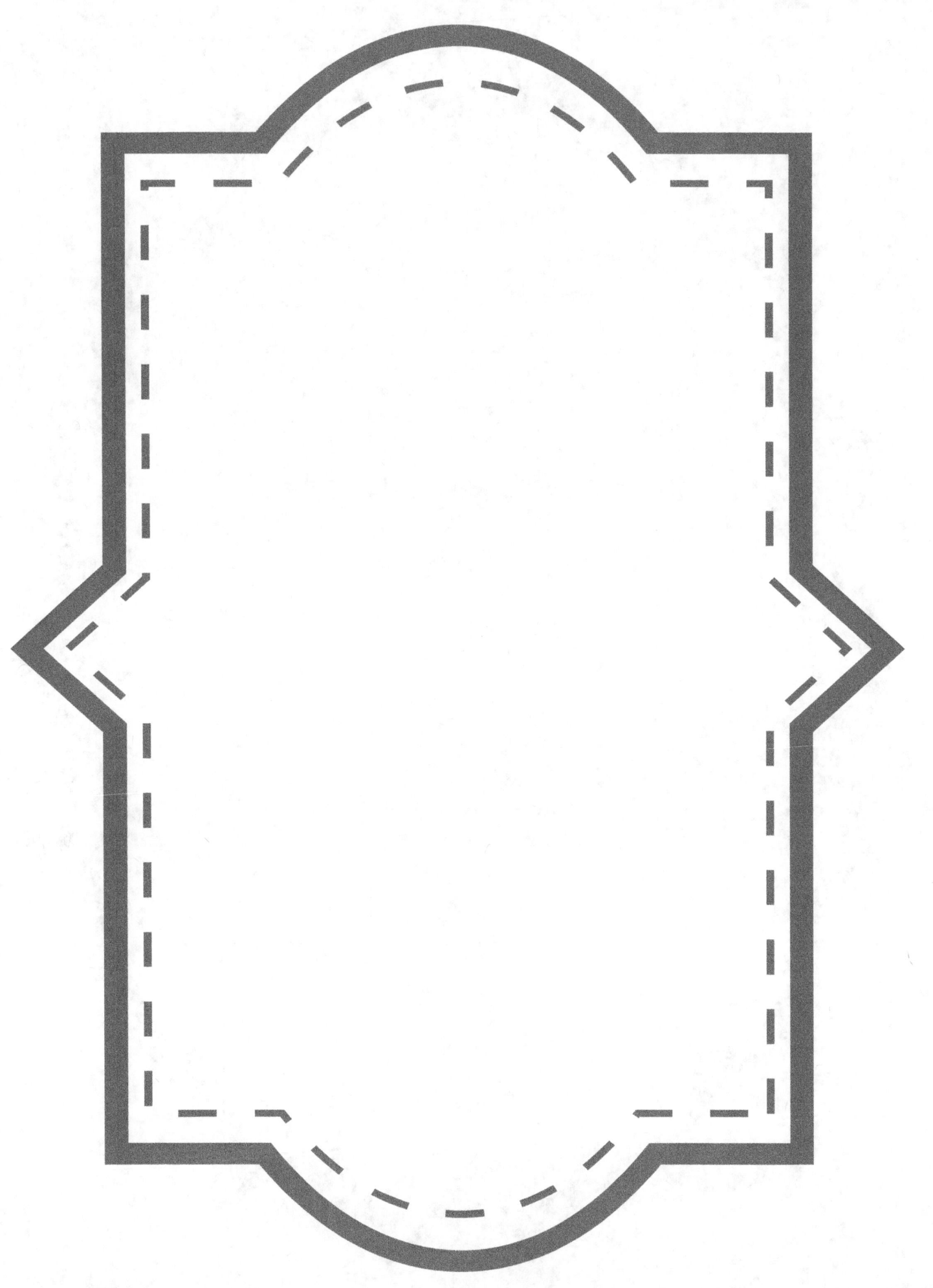

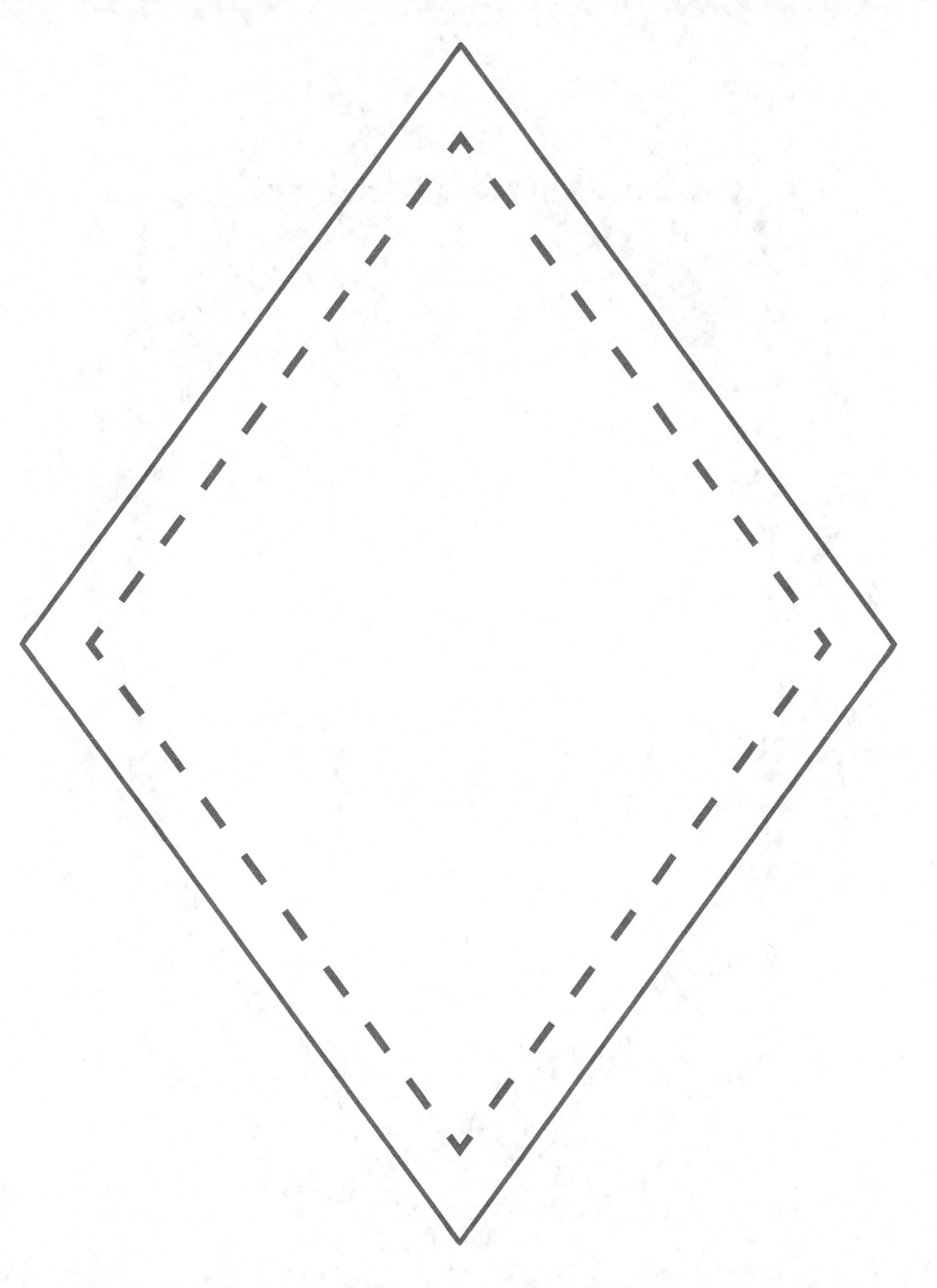

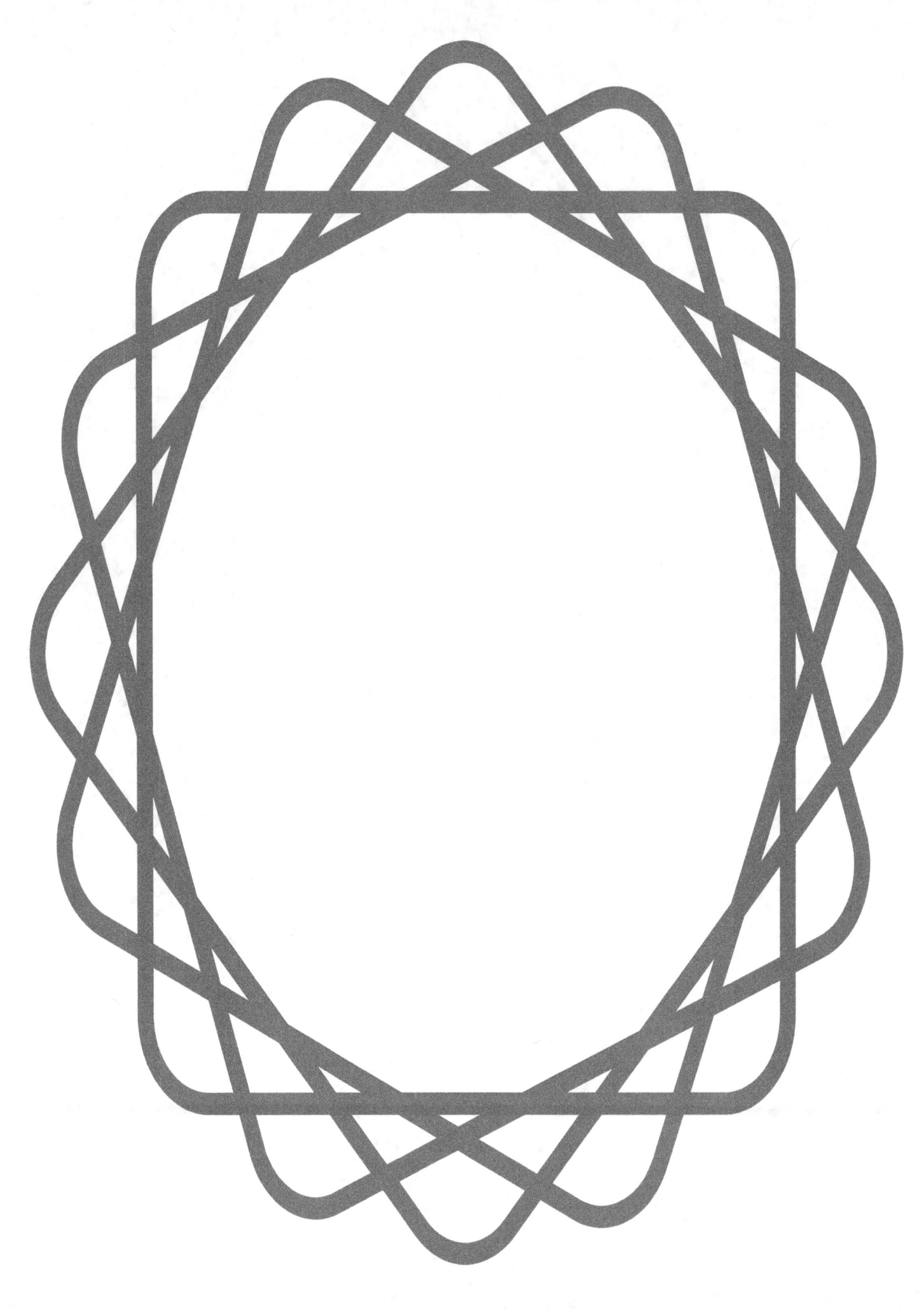

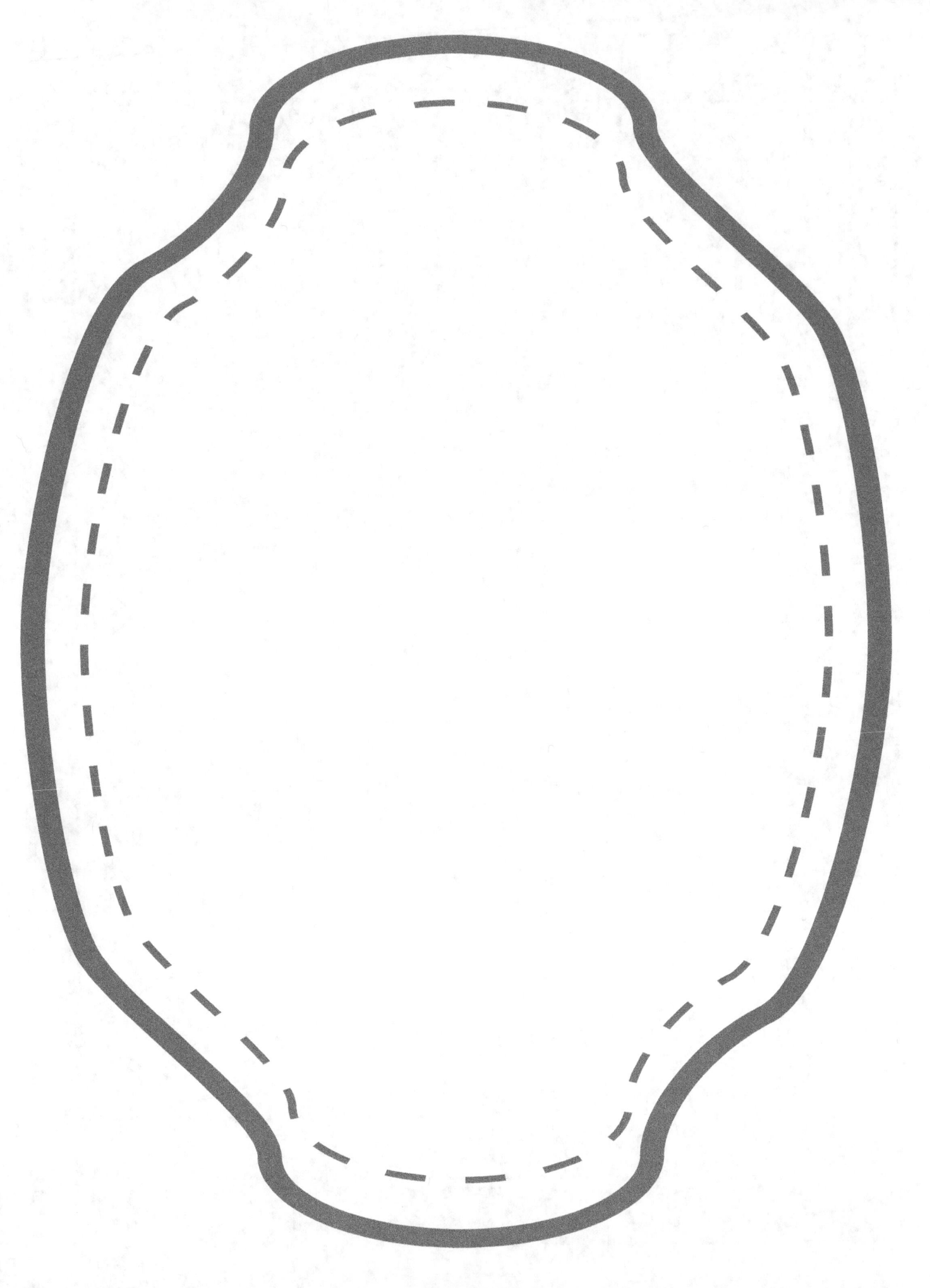

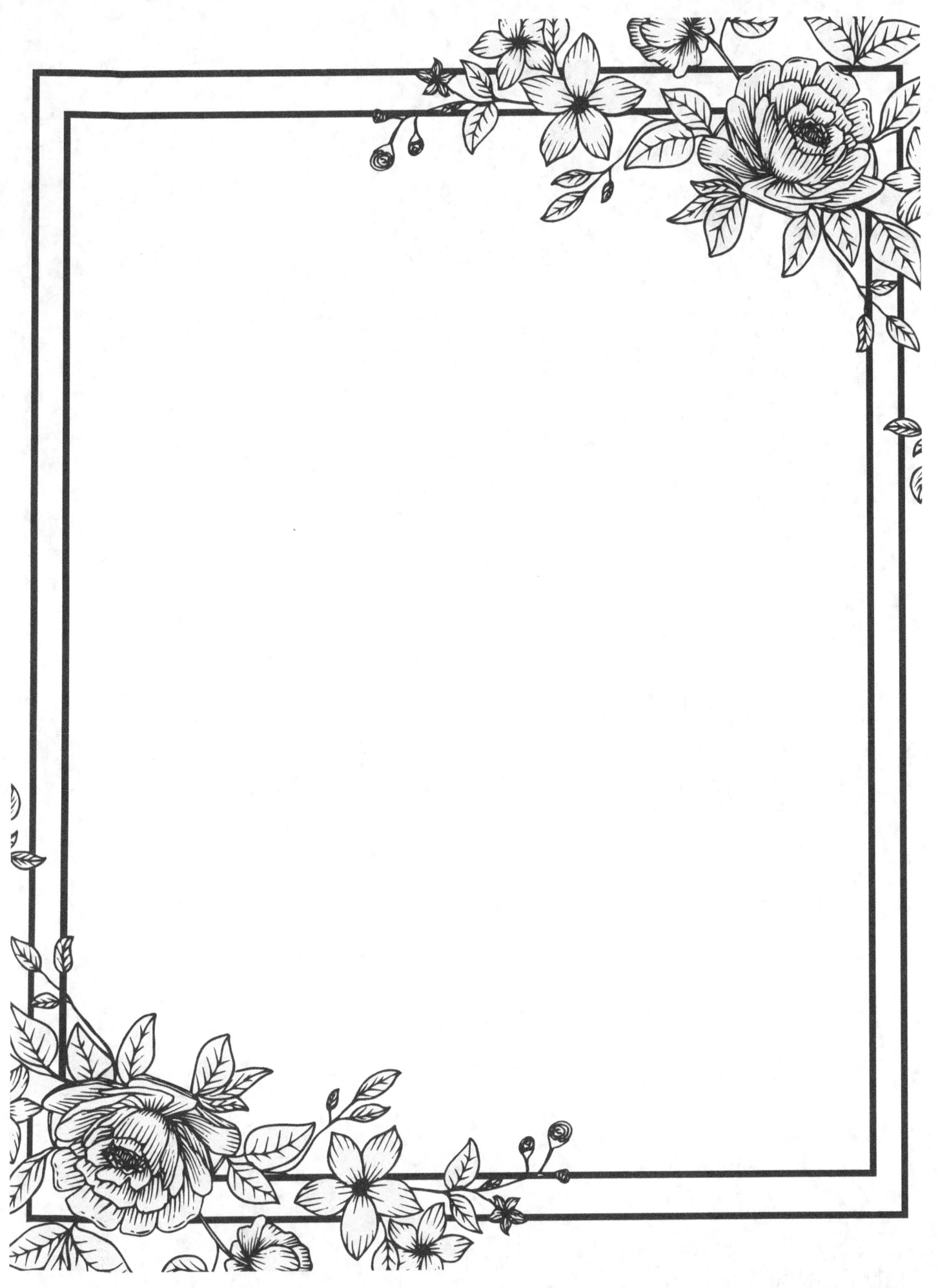

www.ingramcontent.com/pod-product-compliance
Lightning Source LLC
Chambersburg PA
CBHW062334220526
45469CB00008B/2712